How to Argue with Vegans

An analysis of anti-vegan arguments

by

Benny Malone

Cover design and illustration by Richard Watts

@punishedfist on Instagram

Copyright © 2021 Benny Malone

All rights reserved. No part of this publication may be reproduced, stored in a retrieval system, or transmitted, in any form, or by any means electronic, mechanical, recording or otherwise without permission in writing from the publisher, except by a reviewer who may quote brief passages in a review.

Disclaimer - This book is not intended to replace any treatment or advice from medical professionals.

Acknowledgements

Special thanks go to my wife Amanda for her support and encouragement. Thanks to Kylie Mitchell, Charles Horn, Richard Watts, Kevin Watkinson and too many other friends and family to mention for suggestions and valuable discussions and conversations over the years and for particular help in reviewing the manuscript.

Contents

Introduction

Chapter One – Thought Terminating Cliches
Chapter Two – Discussions
Chapter Three – Psychology
Chapter Four – Logical Fallacies
Chapter Five – Variables
Chapter Six – Reflexive Arguments
Chapter Seven – The Case For Veganism

"You never change things by fighting against the existing reality.
To change something, build a new model that makes the old model obsolete."

- Buckminster Fuller

Introduction

The aim of this book is to examine and analyse arguments and responses to veganism that are commonly brought up when a case for veganism or animal rights is being made. By looking at these arguments I hope to provide some tools for their classification and analysis. My hope is that this will be useful for vegans making a case for veganism and defending animal rights and for those who aren't vegan yet to gain insight from a vegan perspective.

I have structured the book in the order I have observed arguments and discussions develop. In analysing online discussions or conversing with people about veganism certain patterns can be observed and many questions are in the frequently asked question category. You can even notice various trends over time and how some arguments become more common or fall out of favour. A number of forces make some arguments more popular than others. Vegans making arguments for veganism can focus on various areas, the media can push certain narratives in response to current affairs and the animal exploitation industries can react to these or work on damage limitation and PR exercises or involve themselves in litigation against whistle-blowers or vegan alternatives. The latter has led to arguments about the labelling of vegan products being amongst the most prominent arguments presently.

The order of anti-vegan arguments in the book follows a progression of not wanting to discuss the topic all the way through to engaging with the issues in an increasingly relevant and valid way. This entails adopting more of the premises of the arguments making up a case for veganism. It can be seen as a progression from outright denial to accepting animal sentience and moral consideration and accepting many environmental and health arguments, but coming to different conclusions. The differing degrees of relevance and acceptance of 'vegan' premises dictates the sort of arguments that will be used against being vegan.

I have divided this progression into the following chapters. In Chapter One we look at Thought Terminating Cliches. These attempt to use platitudes and cliches in place of examining arguments and are a way to avoid the issue altogether. In Chapter Two we examine the definition of veganism and how this can frame discussions and how we can have more productive conversations. In Chapter Three we look at Cognitive Biases and the psychology of meat eating. These are to do with the thinking process itself and how we think. Chapter Four looks at logical fallacies and how so many anti-vegan arguments are full of faulty reasoning. Chapter Five examines what I have found to be a key tool in looking at what the most relevant arguments are – the variables of an argument. Chapter Six is divided into several parts where I analyse what I have called 'reflexive arguments'. As the name suggests these are attempts to turn vegan arguments back on veganism to argue against it. Many of these arguments are fallacies too but are at least more relevant and so of a different category to fallacies of relevance that are the most common type in Chapter Four. As the arguments get more relevant they adopt more and more vegan premises until we are at a stage where the supposed anti-vegan arguments are actually things that can and should be addressed within veganism. Chapter Seven therefore looks at arguments that are more to do with putting veganism into practice and the issues that arise around this. Ideally these issues would be discussed and solved by vegans because it is then that they are taken seriously and not merely weaponised as anti-vegan talking points from people who are not avoiding animal use and slaughter. I hope the reader finds the book a useful framework for beginning to categorise and answer the questions that arise around veganism and offers some insight into an approach to seeking solutions and defending animal rights and veganism.

Chapter One

Thought Terminating Cliches

The initial problem with talking to people about veganism is that people do not want to talk about veganism.

Specifically, they do not really want to get into discussions about how animals are used and slaughtered.
People will say things like 'don't show me, I don't want to see that' or 'I don't want to know' when confronted with images of slaughterhouses. These phrases and platitudes are known as **thought terminating cliches**. (1)
The most common you will see employed by people when veganism or animal use is the topic are -

- Live and let live
- Each to their own
- It's a personal choice
- Agree to disagree
- You do you
- Circle of life
- Humane slaughter
- Don't judge
- Can't we all just get along?

They are 'thought terminating' because they aim to stop any further inquiry, development, or criticism of the thought. They want to use the phrase and for that to be an end to the conversation before it can even begin.

A thought-terminating cliche is a commonly used phrase, sometimes passing as folk wisdom, used to propagate cognitive dissonance (discomfort experienced when one simultaneously holds two or more conflicting cognitions, e.g. ideas, beliefs, values or emotional reactions). Though the phrase in and of itself may be valid in certain contexts, its application as a means of dismissing dissent or justifying fallacious logic is what makes it thought-terminating.

The term was popularized by Robert Jay Lifton in his 1956 book Thought Reform and the Psychology of Totalism. Lifton said, "The language of the totalist environment is characterized by the thought-terminating cliche. The most far-reaching and complex of human problems are compressed into brief, highly reductive, definitive-sounding phrases, easily memorized and easily expressed. These become the start and finish of any ideological analysis."

I remember attending a vegan pop-up dinner party years ago and non-vegans who were there made it clear to me at the outset that 'it is a matter of personal choice' and by this they were making it known they didn't want to debate the issues. 'Personal Choice Vegans' are their favourite type of vegan. The non-vegan wants to make it a personal choice because if we 'agree to disagree' then there is no development or evolution of the discussion. There is no exchange of ideas. The debate is terminated before it can get going with these phrases.

They are cliches too because they are unexamined platitudes for the most part. Have people really thought about what they are saying when it comes to 'live and let live' when it comes to animal use and slaughter? The non-vegan will also happily tell you that they are 'fine with you being vegan' and 'have nothing against vegans' and may pay lip service to the idea of not using and slaughtering animals. Why would they be against someone having a personal dietary preference (as they mischaracterise veganism)? It's because if it's just a personal choice like any other there is no judgement or discrimination of ideas. One choice is as good as another because the choices are personal, like any other choice on a menu of consumer items. It's not for anyone to judge another's choice or taste. Basically they want to make it clear they are fine with you being vegan as long as you leave them alone and it's an attempt at getting reciprocation from the vegan to be 'fine' with *their* 'personal choice'. It can also be an attempt to make the vegan seem unreasonable, interfering and moralising. You aren't fine with people living their lives and making their choices? How unreasonable of you! The playbook of tobacco, oil and fast food companies all frame everything as Consumer Freedom and its enemy as the 'Nanny State'. This framing has had disastrous consequences for public health. Of course, vegans want people to make personal choices, just not those that promote animal use and slaughter. They want people to use the power of choice for a better alternative.

Forcing views!

This is the first hurdle when discussing veganism, people seek comfort in the status quo and don't like being challenged.
If there is a risk they will get into a debate they want to shut it down at the inception and even be pre-emptive like

my fellow diner and make it clear they don't want a discussion on ethics.

The subject can be uncomfortable because it is a moral judgement, it is on a subject of exploitation and slaughter of animals which is upsetting to most people when they see the reality.

If people came to a conclusion that they were wrong about animal use and slaughter and that it would be better to use alternatives that avoid this, then the costs to them can vary. It depends how invested they are in defending those arguments and how much they identify with the arguments. If it's your career it is a bigger ship to turn round than if you are someone who has no financial incentive to exploit animals. Psychologically too there is investment in identifying as a meat eater. The more a person is invested in identifying with the arguments the harder it is for them to abandon them. This is true for any ideology and is where **cognitive dissonance** comes in. **Slothful induction** can mean people are slow to connect ideas and slow to change. There is also the **'Sunk Cost Fallacy'** where so much has been invested in an idea or practice that people continue with it even though it may be a bad idea to do so. Rather than 'cutting one's losses' we continue because we have already put in time, money or effort into the thing we are defending.

As Upton Sinclair said – 'It is difficult to get a man to understand something when his salary depends upon his not understanding it.' The more someone is invested in an argument, whether that is through identity or actual money, the more difficult it may be for them to change their mind and the more likely they will have sunk costs into their position.

People will also want to highlight problems in other

countries, with other types of animal exploitation and killing that most people in their society don't approve of or support. This is another type of thought terminating cliche that just seeks to keep the discussion in those areas. If a celebrity consistently points to these areas that no one agrees with anyway they don't have to challenge their audience or themselves and can stay in their comfort zone. Just like the vegan that people prefer is the *non-challenging quiet vegan*, this celebrity type will be popular with them also. Everyone can just carry on business as usual, make no personal changes in practical or philosophical terms and maintain their comfort level. For example Ricky Gervais is notorious for highlighting areas that no one, or hardly anyone, in the U.K. would agree with anyway. He doesn't maintain the same energy for all areas of animal use and isn't as iconoclastic as he thinks. Do you think celebrities that actually challenged people on the areas of animal use and slaughter they were complicit in would maintain their popularity or appeal to those complicit in those acts? People want to abrogate responsibility and say they are against things they aren't involved in anyway. It is harder to look inward and at our own lives.

"Everyone thinks of changing the world. But no one thinks of changing themselves."
– Leo Tolstoy

"I always thought someone should do something about that.
Then I realised I am someone."

Going vegan was being tired of my own excuses.

Many non-vegan writers do understand these points and

have written about understanding veganism as the more moral position but say they are lacking 'will power' or commitment. (2)

Distancing – "I could never do that!"

Not all such characterisations of vegans will be unflattering. In fact the other way to create distance and therefore justify your own inaction or attitude is to put vegans on a pedestal.
This may be more unconscious than the overt hatred of vegans that is sometimes displayed. Perhaps there is genuine admiration for vegans. But if it is exaggerated then vegans are made out to be superhuman with greater resolve and willpower than the 'average human'.
Therefore, such reserves are beyond the ability of mere mortals like them!
By identifying a superhuman effort or character trait that they say is needed to be vegan people create a comfortable distance between themselves and the change that would be required to be vegan. Be careful with this over-admiration and with non-vegans who 'could never do what you are doing'.
I have been likened to an ascetic monk for being vegan but flattery gets us nowhere.
Vegan literature is filled with tales of people who never thought they would be vegan and who thought it was taking things too far and too extreme. I was one of those. Placing vegans or veganism as an unreachable goal is done so you have an excuse to not even try. Maybe this is where the myth of the 'perfect vegan' or 'being 100% vegan' comes from. Make veganism more difficult than it is and no one can blame you for not being able to run a marathon. (see Nirvana fallacy in chapter four). The idea of privilege is also used to create distance to the goal. A false narrative

of vegans being only from privileged backgrounds erases the diversity of vegans who come from all backgrounds and demographics. (3) This characterisation may be another early stage in terminating any potential for change.

Distancing is also done in terms of time. A future solution such as a technological fix or invention is often proposed when veganism is mentioned. This deferment of taking any action until an undefined future date is another way of creating distance. Rather than take the present day best available option of veganism they say they will take advantage of animal flesh alternatives in the future to avoid acting in the present. They will set the bar too high for some metrics that an alternative to animal exploitation will have to meet and of course no current options are good enough compared to the future ideal. They may also say 'we will look back in horror' on how animals are used in the present day. If you can realise this now why not look upon things as they are now?

As Jan Dutkiewicz has observed, it may be the fact that veganism is an available practical option that means there is more pushback.
He writes ''Modern animal agriculture kills tens of billions of animals every year, making it the quantitatively largest form of violence in human history. And it's all so humans can eat and food producers (mostly agri-capitalist corporations) can profit. But that's also all it is: Food. With a combination of changing how we produce food, what we construe as desirable food, and what consumers buy, we could have a 'vegan' world that looks very much like our current world. People would just need to slightly tweak their behaviour. And I think that's the problem. All of these huge claims about accessibility, corporate control of the food system, etc. apply to our current food and political-economic system as well - but that system could just exist

without animals. You don't need a revolution. So on the one hand people might not want that sort of system (they want an alternative food system) or they might not want the current political-economic system (with good reason), but those are arguments about the systems, not veganism. So ultimately I think it's the possibility of an animal-free world that's a lot like our current world - the fact that it's actually feasible - if only people make small changes is where the pushback comes from. You don't need to own a house to change your oven from gas to electric, you don't need to be able to afford an EV, you don't need to bring down the agrifood system. It's the one huge change that's actually feasible. And so for whatever reason - pleasure is likely central, as are habit and tradition - there is this major pushback that makes it seem like this is some monumental change.
I think people make veganism / animal-free food production into this massive issue because it's actually a feasible change within the parameters of our currently-existing system. Call it the vegan paradox."

If it is something you could actually be doing then to avoid it you need to create distance whether that is psychological or in time. This is where the psychological pressure comes from because people know it is achievable. So they distance themselves from it by elevating or denigrating vegans or saying a solution is further away in time or accessibility.

Saving face and leaving an honourable way out.

Vegan advocacy is about fostering personal, societal and systemic change.
One tip with discussing anything where you want people to change their minds is giving them the space they need to

do so. A person backed into a corner by logic may be utterly defeated in your internet debate. But have they got any room to manoeuvre? Or would a climb down be almost impossible?

We may win the argument but lose the person.

People are not scared vegans are wrong. They are scared they may be right.
People are not worried vegans are wrong and that they will really harm more animals or wreak environmental destruction. They are worried vegans are right and what this implies for their own lifestyle and ideology.

More ways in which people don't want to consider the actual arguments on their own merit is by **shooting the messenger**.

If they can characterise vegans as eccentrics, or otherwise ridicule them (the fallacy is **appeal to ridicule**) then the credibility of the speaker or rather the character is attacked and then they can satisfy themselves that the arguments do not have to be dealt with.

This is why people will jump on the slightest thing you say that they will take offence to and use that as their get-out of the debate card.

Regardless of whether someone is right or wrong to use your behaviour as an excuse, I think we should seek to minimise the potential for any misunderstandings and any hostility from our side being used as an excuse. Tom Regan advised that we shouldn't be that excuse that people will use. (4) We may be held to a higher standard in our conduct because we are trying to change people's minds. People arguing against us may have no interest in maintaining any civility.

Defend your position

People can't really defend their position so seek to deny there is a debate at all through thought terminating cliches and pre-emptively dismissing grounds for a discussion by employing cognitive biases and logical fallacies.

Arguments accusing people of hypocrisy are common at this early stage of discussions. If personal choice argument is not employed because it's accepted that it is a moral issue then this is likely to be what is employed as the 'leveller'. If the 'personal choice' makes all choices personal and so irrelevant in that way, so too does the hypocrisy argument - everyone is as bad as the other and every choice is as bad as the other.

Table Talk

The intent with 'personal choice' and suchlike arguments is to take morality off the table. Veganism is the effort to put it on the table.
The arguments about hypocrisy and 'vegans cause various harms too' accepts moral arguments but the attempt is to create a **paralysis of choice** and again defend taking no action and the status quo. Just like a thought terminating cliche, these become 'morality terminating cliches' to try and create moral equivalence. This is why you could say you are vegan for the most bizarre reason imaginable but as long as it is for personal health reasons and you aren't proselytising the other person will generally be fine with it. Add in any element of morality and suddenly it is no longer a private matter.

Assigning you your reasons you are vegan!

The reasons your opponents will say you are vegan are never actually why you are vegan. It's said to be virtue signalling, to feel superior etc. Not actually because you simply want to avoid animal use and slaughter. If the real reason you yourself are vegan is acknowledged, then that is the discussion point that has to be addressed. This is the area that people want to avoid though. They purposefully assign illogical, emotive or malicious motives to vegans to avoid addressing the real reason and to shoot the messenger to destroy credibility. The stereotype of the preachy, loud vegan is another tool to prevent any discussion. At this stage of discussions there can be a lot of **tone policing** which is another way to shoot the messenger, address their 'tone' as 'angry' or 'preachy' and avoid addressing the real core of the argument.

It's not true that people don't like talking about vegans. In fact they love to concentrate on vegans rather than the exploitation and slaughter of animals. Media platforms love a good vegan story and they are delighted with the extra engagement they bring in reactions and comments compared to their usual posts. If people can concentrate on vegans and shooting the messenger it means they don't have to address how animals are used and on the animals themselves. Can we as vegans remove ourselves from the equation? Only as far as possible. Advocating for an end to animal exploitation requires humans communicating with other humans who are supporting animal use and slaughter.

People will say ''so you think I'm a bad person?''
No, I think you are a good person, which is why I respect you enough to think you might want to avoid animal use and slaughter.

Notes to Chapter One

Thanks to J.D. Mumma for introducing me to the term 'thought terminating cliches'.

1. From Wikipedia's now deleted page on Thought Terminating Cliches http://jorgenmodin.net/index_html/wikpedias-now-deleted-page-on-thought-terminating-cliche

2. Nathan Nobis - https://www.nathannobis.com/2020/07/checking-check-your-privilege-for.html

3. See David Mitchell's article for a non-vegan perspective that is insightful on why they actually find vegans vexing.
https://www.theguardian.com/commentisfree/2018/dec/09/my-beef-with-vegans-says-more-about-me-than-them-david-mitchell

Sam De Brito also details his thoughts on how he used to find vegans annoying https://www.smh.com.au/opinion/confessions-of-a-vegan-20140726-zx84p.html

4. 'The last thing other animals need is another reason not to care about them. How we act towards other people can provide just such a reason. Being rude or judgmental doesn't help any nonhuman. A coping technique I use (to quell my impatience, when I feel it bubbling-up in my throat) is to think of the people who ask questions I've been asked hundreds of times as mirrors. Yes, I think of them as mirrors. When I look at them, in other words, what I see is a reflection of who I used to be. Like them, there was a time when I didn't know how other animals were being treated. Like them, there was a time when I knew but didn't care. Like them, there was a time when I knew and cared but not enough to change how I was living. Like them, there was a time when I was . . . them! That's what I try to remind myself. I don't want to come across as self-righteous or arrogant. That would give the questioner another reason not to care about other animals, and I don't want to do that—I don't want to be that reason.' – Tom Regan

From an interview with Carolyn Bailey for AR Zone -
https://arzone.ning.com/profiles/blogs/animal-rights-philosopher-tom

Chapter Two

Discussions

People can be sincere in trying to argue and not realise they are committing fallacies or simply not be aware of all of the facts. All of us have had to learn and *unlearn* various positions and attitudes. However, others will be using deliberate tactics to try and win a debate. They aren't winning on technical terms but are seeking to prejudice listeners or readers towards their arguments by use of various tactics.
Rhetorical tricks aren't in themselves bad but like any tool they can be misused.

Graham's Hierarchy

When it comes to disagreements there is a useful essay written by Paul Graham called 'How to Disagree'. [1] It sets up a hierarchy of best to worst ways to disagree. Similar to hierarchies of quality of evidence, this hierarchy is quality of argument or more specifically, disagreement. It links in with the fallacies we will examine because using fallacies or displaying cognitive bias fits into the hierarchy on a lower level because it's a poorer way to disagree. Better ways as you move up the hierarchy involve actually countering arguments and using facts and addressing the issue or your opponent's argument without relying on the worst forms of discussion.

Graham's Hierarchy of Disagreement:

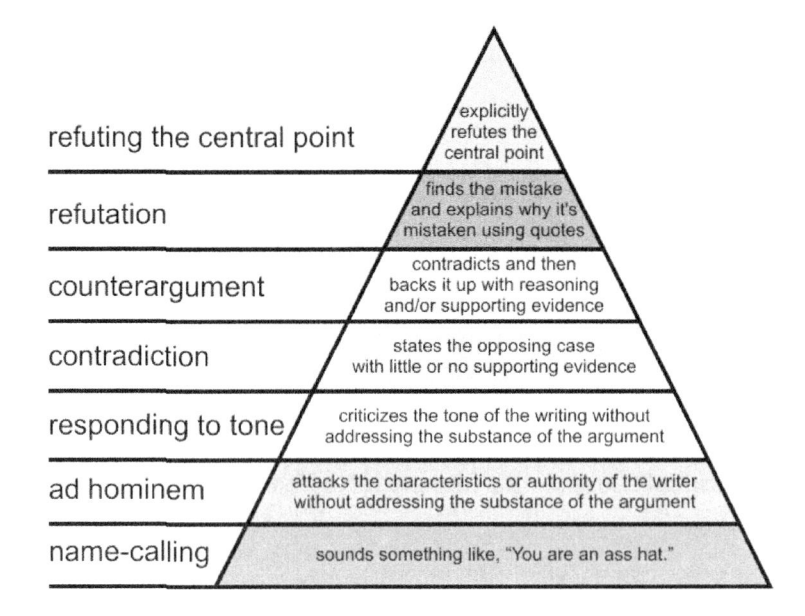

- **refuting the central point** — explicitly refutes the central point
- **refutation** — finds the mistake and explains why it's mistaken using quotes
- **counterargument** — contradicts and then backs it up with reasoning and/or supporting evidence
- **contradiction** — states the opposing case with little or no supporting evidence
- **responding to tone** — criticizes the tone of the writing without addressing the substance of the argument
- **ad hominem** — attacks the characteristics or authority of the writer without addressing the substance of the argument
- **name-calling** — sounds something like, "You are an ass hat."

When you see a disagreement you can analyse it and see where it lies on Graham's hierarchy. The person disagreeing can be guided to using better arguments and ways of disagreeing if they are aware of the hierarchy also. If they refuse to then there is no need to address the lower types of disagreement in a serious discussion.

Debate tactics

Unfortunately, not everyone enters a discussion in good faith and with a familiarity with Graham's Hierarchy or Gorrell's principles for productive discussions. (2) They will employ some debate tactics that the reader should be aware of, from the deliberate use of fallacies to various rhetorical devices.

Sowing Doubt and Concern Trolling

The areas where anti-vegans want to argue may be where they feel they can score points more easily and avoid the weakest areas. It's natural for everyone to want to argue in their best areas if they are trying to win a debate. However amongst anti-vegans there is deliberate use of certain tactics which they have discussed. They say 'ask about oysters' (Denise Minger does this on her blog) and for people to concentrate on areas of more contention – honey, pets, service animals and the like rather than areas a general audience can more easily understand.
They want to avoid areas of certainty and where they should be avoiding animal use even if the 'marginal' areas are actually truly contentious. The areas of exception would prove the rule – that is, they actually make the case for avoiding animal use in the areas of certainty.

Gish Gallop

The Gish gallop is a technique used during debating to try to overwhelm an opponent with as many arguments as possible, without regard for the veracity or validity of the arguments. The term was coined by Eugenie Scott and named after the creationist Duane Gish, who used the technique frequently against proponents of evolution.

Anti-vaxxers will often share lengthy pre-prepared lists of questions about vaccinations to overwhelm opponents. There are several ways of dealing with a Gish Gallop. You do not have to engage anyone acting in such bad faith in a debate. You can ask to address one point and deal solely with that. You can actually address and refute each point in turn, which is obviously very time consuming. Often social media exchanges can involve a battle of sharing links that

neither party will read or have probably not even read themselves. In their haste to debunk veganism, some famous science pages have even shared things which do not support their argument against veganism and actually make a good case against consuming meat and dairy.
The Gish Galloper will produce a long list of questions and expect an answer to each one. They may use an **On The Spot Fallacy** of demanding an immediate answer.
It may bring to mind **Brandolini's law**
"The amount of energy needed to refute bullshit is an order of magnitude bigger than to produce it."

Many of the debate points of a Gish Gallop may actually be arguments that have already been thoroughly refuted. As a lot of the arguments that come up in vegan discussions come up again and again it's clear that people aren't familiar with the answers or that their points have already been refuted, not even necessarily by vegans but by science. A **point refuted a thousand times**, commonly abbreviated as **PRATT**, is an argument that comes up so often that many people do not feel they are worth bothering with. This may be true for some subjects but for veganism I think it is still worth getting the answers to Frequently Asked Questions out there as they may be new to people who simply haven't carried the questions through to their logical conclusions. 'Bingo Cards' for these PRATTS exist for lots of subjects including veganism but will probably be received badly if offered as answers to sincere inquiries. There are 'zombie questions' that pop up again and again no matter how many times you answer them so it's a matter of personal judgement and patience as to where you concentrate your educational efforts and which questions you answer. It can be good to set out the arguments being used as the claim they are making and pair it with the factual response. This takes a good deal of effort but is very satisfying when done well.

Going nuclear

This tactic is used when someone feels cornered in a debate and rather than concede any points they decide to bring the whole epistemological basis of any arguments down with them in a final Samson-esque gesture of destruction! (3)

Rather than continue to accept premises of a regular discussion they will employ a high degree of epistemological doubt which can render any discussion impossible and where no basis for discussion can be agreed upon.

A **creationist escape hatch** is an unarguable, unfalsifiable statement or reply that attempts to end all further discussion. (Rational Wiki)
Escape hatches are a similar tactic. Invoking things which can neither be proven nor disproven reverts a discussion back to a battle of opinions and away from facts and logic. Religious arguments against veganism are of this nature. They are often circular reasoning and appeals to authority with only their own scriptures as evidence.

One of the good ones

'One of the good ones is a phrase that encapsulates the idea of comparing an individual favorably to the other people in their demographic.' (RationalWiki)
Vegans will often play into stereotypes by trying to appeal to non-vegans by appearing to be 'one of the good ones' or 'not one of those type of vegans'. Usually this means that they are the 'personal choice' type who is not vocal about veganism. As we discussed in the chapter on Thought Terminating Cliches, these are the 'good vegans' that

don't disturb the peace of the non-vegan and so are more liked by them. Anyone seeking to advocate for change is going to have to argue against the positions of those who support the exploitation and slaughter of other animals. Usually playing into these stereotypes just reinforces them, doesn't help normalise veganism and helps compound the type of false dilemmas so favoured by those who try to portray vocal vegans as angry extremists and that you can't be both clear and vocal about your position and at same time be friendly and courteous in your advocacy.

Straw Men, Weak Men, and Hollow Men

Scott F. Aikin & John Casey came up with categorisations of Straw Man type arguments that go beyond the most familiar.
A **Straw Man** is when the opponent's argument is constructed in such a way as to be easier to argue against – the 'straw man' is built so it can be knocked down more easily. It may be distorted representation of the opponent's actual position. It may exaggerate or downplay some aspect or otherwise be a bad representation of the argument. The person constructing the straw man can then 'destroy' this argument and claim victory while not really addressing what their opponent is actually saying.
Weak Men – are the worst examples of the opponent's argument or opponent themselves that can be found. In order to once again argue against the weaker position these examples are concentrated on while stronger debaters or arguments are ignored.
Hollow Men – these arguments are dissimilar to straw men in that they aren't distortions of an actual argument but simply are not the argument at all. The hollow Man is purely a made up argument that no one is making the case for that is then argued against.

The preceding examples are all designed to make the person's position stronger by arguing against weak, distorted or non-existent positions. A **Steel Man** argument is the opposite to the straw Man and is when you take the opponent's position and put it in the best form you can. It is good practice for the best forms of argument you are likely to face and for testing how strong your own arguments and counters are.

Related to this is the **principle of charity**. In philosophy and rhetoric, the principle of charity requires interpreting a speaker's statements in the most rational way possible. To do so we are charitable in assuming the rationality and good intentions of the other person. We seek to understand their position and might try to re-state it back to them in the strong steel-manned form that they would consent to being the correct interpretation of their argument. In this way we help prevent distortions and misunderstandings. If we are able to refute their points it will also have been done against the best form of their argument and so we can be confident in a more thorough refutation.

Sniper tactics

This type of tactic is named for the way a sniper has to use cover and distance to be able to attack. In our case it is your arguments that are under fire. Snipers rely on distance and cover. When exposed they lose their tactical advantage and are vulnerable to counter attack. The way to nullify distance and cover is to pin them down by closing any distance and exposing their cover. The book 'Nasty People' by Jay Carter details 'snipers' as one type of passive aggressive person who will insult you but never in a direct and explicit way. To stop them sniping you have to be able to call their bluff and not allow them the plausible deniability of what they meant and to gaslight you. Asking them directly what they mean by their words forces them out into the open. They will either have to put up or shut up, but don't become nasty yourself! If they still want to play at being passive aggressive you just have to keep asking them to be explicit. Most people will tire of this and you have also let them know you are aware of their games. In discussions people will often present any argument they can from one moment to the next while offering no coherent or consistent position of their own. Their aim is to attack your position and avoid revealing their own if possible. Your position will be at least generally known if they know you are vegan. However you do not know the details of their position and their beliefs. It can take a lot of questioning for people to clearly and unambiguously state what their position actually is.

People are often extremely reluctant to be pinned down to committing to a position. If they were to commit to a position they then have to defend it and stick to it for at least as long as they are arguing those points from that position. In debates they may find this disadvantageous for a number of reasons.

1) Perhaps they have not thought through their arguments to their logical conclusions.

They don't actually have the knowledge to defend their position.

2) Perhaps they wish to maintain a Devil's advocate position just to be arguing against yours no matter where the arguments they are using come from or what they would mean the individual would have to believe themselves.

This is related to **Arguments As Soldiers** where any argument will do as long as it is against the opponent's position. One side has a series of arguments and the other side have theirs and the truth of the arguments becomes less important than whether they are directed at the other side.

Once they commit to an answer to a question a position is implied and they would have to stick to it if they wanted to be consistent. They wouldn't be able to contradict their own position in order just to argue with you. They could be offering what other people think about certain issues but if those points aren't their own argument then this should be made clear or it can be intellectually dishonest.
In an absurd example someone may want to argue that plants feel pain in one exchange. In the next they may want to abandon any notion of non-human sentience at all and argue that animals don't feel pain. The tactic is to be throwing arguments at the vegan with no consideration for the implications of their own statements for the position that must therefore be held.

Exchanges with people using these tactics often end with them saying they don't actually care about what they were arguing. They were **Just Asking Questions** – 'a way of attempting to make wild accusations acceptable) by framing them as questions rather than statements. The tactic is closely related to loaded questions or leading questions (which are usually employed when using it), Gish Gallops (when asking a huge number of rapid-fire questions without regard for the answers) and Argumentum ad nauseam (when asking the same question over and over in an attempt to overwhelm
refutations). Sealioning involves jumping into a conversation with endless *polite, reasonable* questions and demands for answers, usually of entry-level topics far below the actual conversation (e.g. "please prove sexism exists"). This tactic differs little from harassment; instead of discussion, the point is to derail discussion, receive criticism (for their ignorance) so as to look like a victim, or to make someone feel overwhelmed and quit talking. It is comparable to running a filibuster (or perhaps a filibustering technique) and preventing anything getting

done.' (4)

In debate forums this was likened to wanting to argue from an amorphous position that shifted from one exchange to the next. The advantage to the sniper who doesn't want to reveal their own position is distance and cover. The way to expose a sniper is to bring them out of cover so they can no longer fire arguments from distance. They are brought into the open on a level playing field and must state their position clearly and be prepared to defend it without contradiction or flip-flopping or changing their argument.

Each statement actually implies a position. It says something about your epistemology, your ethics and logic. If you really want to say plants are sentient and use that as your argument against veganism it means you are committing to sentience as your criteria for moral consideration. So you can't abandon that when it comes to your criteria for moral consideration to animals.

Counters to tactic

Ask people to explicitly state their position.
Ask people what their criteria for moral consideration to animals is.
Ask people what their practical suggestions are as an alternative to yours.
As them if they sincerely believe there is no difference between killing a plant and killing a puppy.

Cautions – we do actually want people to change their minds and abandon fallacious arguments and falsehoods. This is different to flip-flopping continually and even picking arguments up again that have already been disproven.

Schrödinger's Cattle

They may ask 'What will happen to all the animals if everyone goes vegan? Won't they overpopulate? Or where will all the animals go?!'
This is a common question. Vegans will usually answer something like 'the animals that are currently farmed are bred by humans and would not exist otherwise. When more people go vegan over time it will lead to fewer animals being bred and so there is no issue with populations of farmed animals.'

This can then lead them to say 'so vegans want all the animals to go extinct?'
As they were originally asking what happens to the animals this conclusion may genuinely be the first time they have thought about the vegan's answer and the true implications of their question. But their position has shifted dramatically. They have gone from a concern about overpopulation to de-population. So is NOT breeding the animals now their concern? Are they now no longer concerned about animal population explosions and free roaming farmed animals? Obviously given the facts of breeding animals for human use only one concern at a time can be held.

A good Socratic question to respond to '*What will happen to all the animals if everyone goes vegan?*' here is 'where do all the animals come from at the moment?'

The concern naturally often leads to The Logic of the Larder – a phrase coined by animal rights pioneer Henry Salt which we will discuss in chapter four.

Vegan genocide

With the logic of the larder argument I've seen people saying their concern is now the de-population one or in fact the ceasing of breeding animals in order for them to be slaughtered.
Animals are bred to be slaughtered as young as they possibly can be. Think about that for a moment. If the usefulness of an animal's life exceeds any amount of time on this Earth then it represents a loss to the animal exploiter.

People have said that this hypothetical 'slaughtering of all animals one last time and then not breeding anymore' is a 'vegan genocide' of animals. As opposed to the continuous cycle of breeding and slaughtering that you want to continue in perpetuity? What would you call that?
Of course, as we are always being told 'the world won't go vegan overnight!' So why the sudden contradictory concern for an overnight slaughter of every farmed animal in the world and their disappearance? Of course as in the answer to what would happen to all the animals, the process is gradual on a systemic level. As there are more vegans at a significant population level there is less demand over time for breeding and slaughtering animals.

Do people miss the fact that there is NOT a mink farm in their hometown? Are they wondering where all those non-existent animals are? The question is absurd because the notion of concern for non-existent animals is absurd.

If animals cannot live free *on their own terms* then they should not be bred just to be exploited and killed at the earliest possible convenience for humans. The disingenuousness of saying that this is 'giving animals a life and that's better than no life at all' is staggering. This has to be the greatest post-hoc rationalisation employed by animal eaters. They want to kill and eat animals then pretend that giving animals life through breeding them to be slaughtered at the youngest possible age is their real philanthropic concern. If this was truly a concern why don't they donate to and support animal sanctuaries?

Animal sanctuaries are a sanctuary for animals rescued from the fate you wanted imposed on them as a consumer of animal products.

The tree of the circle of life tho

The following observations are 'debate tactics' and about where we find ourselves in an argument.

Imagine a giant flow chart of vegan arguments.
From the initial question many branches will form.
Some may end in a thought terminating cliche.
Other branches may get stuck in a loop of circular reasoning and question begging.
Other branches may lead to cul de sacs where there is no way out and a person feels cornered. They will react defensively and may use any tactic to try to break free from the confines of a loaded question. They will then resort to going nuclear or escape hatches.
More branches have definitive and well-trodden paths. The most common questions vegans are asked will be in this main branch. The 'what about X?' and 'Why do vegans Y?' questions. These are our FAQS and a computer program could direct questioners to the best answers. There have been Climate Change Bots which did similar on that subject. (5)

These main branches lead to the vegan position that we are making a case for, so the route to get from the question to the answer has to be navigated.

In going vegan, each of us has followed a path through this chart. It could be one branch or many but we have ended at a generally similar position which can be identified as being vegan – opposition and avoidance of animal exploitation as per the vegan definition.

The usefulness of picturing such a flow chart is not just so we can reel off ready-made answers. In a genuine process we are coming to those conclusions through logic and science and sound moral reasoning. We may map how the flow chart branches however and see 'where' we are on it. If the flow chart has led to the argument people are making against veganism then we at least know which area we are in and on which branch. This categorisation can show family resemblances amongst the questions and answers. We may recognise patterns which will help identify what the issue is and what solutions there are to the problems.

I have hopes someone more tech-savvy than me may one day draw up such a flow chart of all the many branches of vegan arguments.

I noticed patterns amongst the most common questions about veganism.

These have also changed over time. Most recently at the time of writing July 2020 almost every article on social media that had vegans or plant based food as a topic had many people in comments sections asking 'Why do vegans want to make their food look or taste like meat?' Perhaps there are cycles of which questions get posed the most and some can go viral. It's possible these questions are more popular due to more vegan product launches and the advertising for these.

I have also noticed that there are different types of questions from different demographics – differences in religion, politics and livelihood greatly determine the type of questions the person will ask and they have favourites.

I find it useful to know where I am in a discussion so I can keep referring back to the point I was actually trying to make and see how far the discussion might have strayed. It can be useful to have a general sense of where the questions could be heading and also in which area the discussion is taking place – are the concerns philosophical, logical or practical? Are you talking about health, the environment, public health or ethics?

 Sometimes people might ask for help in a debate and although you are willing to help make a case for veganism, if you are not careful you could end up thinking 'is this really my argument?' There have been times when I've been discussing issues with someone and it has strayed so far from the original area of discussion that my interlocutor is assuming I'm going to have to defend positions that aren't my own or sometimes vegans who want back up want you to adopt and defend their position. If it isn't your area of expertise and not your own sincerely
held position then you don't have to make a case for it or defend it. Ask yourself 'is this *my* argument?' If it isn't you can re-direct the conversation to the position you actually are defending. You may also get bogged down in discussing the minutiae of minor details that have little impact on your overall argument. Ask yourself if it's worth spending time in certain areas of discussion. If it is a matter that can be settled with reference to facts there is not much more you can do after you have provided your sources. It may be time to move on and re-focus on what your main argument is.
If you have found yourself lost along one of the branches and amongst a dense thicket of overwhelming detail then this may be deliberate on the part of the other person.

These sorts of arguments can be part of a communications strategy called "precisionism," a term coined by Matthew Hayek NYU Asst. Professor of Environmental Studies. (6)

'To avoid the full hammer of regulation, he says, some industries can get specific and pedantic in order to distract from their share of emissions and their societal responsibility to mitigate. In a 2018 Science analysis of 570 studies using data from about 38,700 farms, for instance, environmental scientist Joseph Poore and agricultural scientist Thomas Nemecek found that food production is responsible for 26 percent of all global emissions, with beef production making up the largest share."

This is often seen on social media when farmers will want to concentrate on specifics that don't affect the overall picture. They zoom in on whether almonds require a lot of water or how much soy is used to make soy milk rather than taking all variables into account, including animal use and slaughter, land use, full life-cycle analysis and environmental concerns. When all plant milks are better in every conceivable metric compared to dairy then this puts the overall picture into perspective. Once this is acknowledged then the discussion on which plant milk is best and the pros and cons of each can be discussed, with the knowledge that they are all better than dairy. (7) (8)

Definitions

"If you wish to converse with me, define your terms." - Voltaire

I think if people understood the definition of veganism they would think more about what they are arguing against and also implicit in this what they are arguing for when they argue with vegans.

Many simple misunderstandings and misconceptions could be prevented if people had a better understanding of what veganism is – it is not a diet, it is not environmentalism, and what the focus of veganism and the claims as to what areas it covers it makes.
This does require the principle of charity in interpreting the definition. We are interpreting the general spirit of the definition but people will like to argue over extreme details. Pretending not to understand this definition and how to apply it seems disingenuous to me.

The Vegan Society (U.K.) defines veganism as

"A philosophy and way of living which seeks to exclude—as far as is possible and practicable—all forms of exploitation of, and cruelty to, animals for food, clothing or any other purpose; and by extension, promotes the development and use of animal-free alternatives for the benefit of animals, humans and the environment. In dietary terms it denotes the practice of dispensing with all products derived wholly or partly from animals."

I'm a fan of this definition because it is practical and succinct. For a great history of the definition and why it was felt it was needed see A Candid Hominid. (9)

If veganism is framed correctly from the outset many of the misunderstandings that arise can be avoided. I think Kristy Alger does a particularly good job of this in her book 'Five Essays For Freedom'. Noting the distinction between practical and practicable (the latter is when something is able to be put into practice successfully) ''makes allowances for those areas of human life where an impact upon other animals cannot be avoided whilst establishing the framework necessary for animal advocates in their

struggle for change. As a result targeting the individual whose circumstances may necessitate a continued use of animals is avoided.'' (As in the case of absolute necessity of medications for example). If this was more widely understood then many futile arguments could be avoided. ''Practicable veganism brings the focus to the social, economic and political systems that perpetuate the exploitation of other animals. In turn this avoids blaming disempowered individuals and communities for systems they were not responsible for creating. Thus, veganism becomes an ethical standpoint against the politics of animal exploitation without further entrenching the marginalisation of disadvantaged individuals and communities.'' If the many non-vegan Leftist critics of veganism understood this they could start to help promote veganism rather than continuing to spread their own misunderstanding of it as an argument to continue animal exploitation. (10)
One way I define veganism simply is to say that it is a position against the commodity status and exploitation of other animals. I find this clears up a lot of confusion about being 'part-time vegan' and those sort of questions.

Steven Novella of 'Skeptic's Guide To The Universe' had a great question about science.

"What do you think science is? There's nothing magical about science. It is simply a systematic way for carefully and thoroughly observing nature and using consistent logic to evaluate results. Which part of that exactly do you disagree with? Do you disagree with being thorough? Using careful observation? Being systematic? Or using consistent logic?"

I think when this is adapted to ask people what it is exactly that they find disagreement with veganism it can be a powerful exploratory question.

What part of avoiding animal use and slaughter do you disagree with exactly?
What part of using oat milk instead of subjecting cows, goats and sheep to exploitation and slaughtering their offspring to take the milk do you disagree with?
What part of minimising animal use do you disagree with? Veganism is simply using a non-animal alternative where available. As in the case of not using cosmetic products tested on animals. What principle are you following when, all things being equal, you insist on animal testing or slaughter as the only unique variable?

We can also ask people 'What would change your mind about the subject?' as a test of their dogmatism and refusal to acknowledge facts.
The answer reveals a lot about how willing people are to reassess their arguments.
If the answer is 'evidence' what evidence for animal sentience would change your mind?
What evidence for the environmental impact of animal use do you require?
What standard of evidence for the health of plant based diets would you accept?

The scientific consensus is with plant based diets in these areas and with the sentience of animals.

Notes to Chapter Two

(1) Paul Graham's original article which I recommend reading can be found here –
http://www.paulgraham.com/disagree.html
(2) This is another useful resource for some guidelines on having productive and fair discussions.
https://thoughtcatalog.com/brandon-gorrell/2011/03/how-to-have-a-rational-discussion/
(3) https://www.psychologytoday.com/gb/blog/believing-bull/201109/kaboom-going-nuclear-in-argument
(4) see - https://thelogicofscience.com/2020/05/31/the-problem-with-just-asking-questions/
(5) https://www.popsci.com/science/article/2010-11/twitter-chatbot-trolls-web-tweeting-science-climate-change-deniers/
(6) https://undark.org/2021/02/03/beef-industry-funding-climate/
(7) https://www.bbc.co.uk/news/science-environment-46654042
(8) https://www.health.harvard.edu/staying-healthy/plant-milk-or-cows-milk-which-is-better-for-you#:~:text=Plant-based%20milks%20are%20superior,be%20the%20way%20to%20go.
(9) http://www.candidhominid.com/p/vegan-history.html
(10) Five Essays For Freedom by Kristy Alger (Revolutionaries press 2020)

Chapter Three

Psychology

"Because we have viewed other animals through the myopic lens of our self-importance, we have misperceived who and what they are. Because we have repeated our ignorance, one to the other, we have mistaken it for knowledge."
- Tom Regan

Cognitive Biases

In this section we will look at cognitive biases and some psychological aspects of animal use. In a later chapter we will look at fallacies which are errors in reasoning in arguments in contrast to the systemic processes of thinking. A cognitive bias is an error in thinking which does not come from the structure of a logical argument. Rather it comes from the process of thinking itself. In trying to make sense of our physical, emotional and cognitive environment we are subject to systematic errors from our own thinking processes.
Thinking about thinking is one of the most difficult things we can do. Philosophers down the ages have noted how 'the eye cannot see itself' and 'the sword cannot cut itself'. We are used to examining external objects but turning the gaze inwards from object to subject is more difficult. We can be quick to notice the errors of others or their patterns of thought but a certain level of detachment is required for more honest introspection. We can try to observe our thoughts and feelings but we are not objective observers. Becoming more aware that we may be mistaken in our reasoning can help us be more alert in identifying potential pitfalls in our thinking. Once you become aware that there are certain psychological processes that the brain carries

out, this awareness can help identify them. We can then take measures to rectify any errors as far as we can and improve our reasoning. We can also see where other people may be subject to cognitive biases.

A humbling dictum to keep in mind is this - "The first principle is that you must not fool yourself - and you are the easiest person to fool." - Richard Feynman

I will go through some of the biases I have come across when discussing veganism. As always these are good to know about to help identify and analyse our own and other's arguments. We should seek to eliminate any harmful biases that impede our reasoning and judgement. We want to use the strongest arguments at our disposal. Critical thinking can help everyone strengthen their arguments and in a subject like veganism this means more time to deal with important issues. There are many more cognitive biases and psychological factors than I can cover here so I limit the discussion to those that most frequently occur when the subject of veganism comes up.

Francis Bacon Tho

Francis Bacon (1561-1626) was one of the earliest thinkers to identify what we now call cognitive biases.
He categorised errors in mental processing into four Idols of the Mind: Idols of the Tribe, Idols of the Cave, Idols of the Marketplace, and Idols of the Theatre.

''The **Idols of the Tribe** have their foundation in human nature itself, and in the tribe or race of men. For it is a false assertion that the sense of man is the measure of things. On the contrary, all perceptions as well of the sense as of the mind are according to the measure of the individual and not according to the measure of the universe. And the human understanding is like a false mirror, which, receiving rays irregularly, distorts and discolours the nature of things by mingling its own nature with it.''

''The **Idols of the Cave** are the idols of the individual man. For everyone (besides the errors common to human nature in general) has a cave or den of his own, which refracts and discolours the light of nature, owing either to his own proper and peculiar nature; or to his education and conversation with others; or to the reading of books, and the authority of those whom he esteems and admires; or to the differences of impressions, accordingly as they take place in a mind preoccupied and predisposed or in a mind indifferent and settled; or the like. So that the spirit of man (according as it is meted out to different individuals) is in fact a thing variable and full of perturbation, and governed as it were by chance. Whence it was well observed by Heraclitus that men look for sciences in their own lesser worlds, and not in the greater or common world.''

One is reminded of Shelley's words 'Life, like a dome of many-coloured glass, Stains the white radiance of Eternity'
The Cave has been used in philosophy and religion as a metaphor for the cave-like nature of the human skull. So we can think of these phenomena as being in our own heads. Plato's allegory of the cave is instructive here too.

''There are also Idols formed by the intercourse and association of men with each other, which I call **Idols of the Market Place**, on account of the commerce and consort of men there. For it is by discourse that men associate, and words are imposed according to the apprehension of the vulgar. And therefore the ill and unfit choice of words wonderfully obstructs the understanding. Nor do the definitions or explanations wherewith in some things learned men are wont to guard and defend themselves, by any means set the matter right. But words plainly force and overrule the understanding, and throw all into confusion, and lead men away into numberless empty controversies and idle fancies.''

''Lastly, there are Idols which have immigrated into men's minds from the various dogmas of philosophies, and also from wrong laws of demonstration. These I call **Idols of the Theatre**, because in my judgment all the received systems are but so many stage plays, representing worlds of their own creation after an unreal and scenic fashion. Nor is it only of the systems now in vogue, or only of the ancient sects and philosophies, that I speak; for many more plays of the same kind may yet be composed and in like artificial manner set forth; seeing that errors the most widely different have nevertheless causes for the most part alike. Neither again do I mean this only of entire systems, but also of many principles and axioms in science, which by tradition, credulity, and negligence have come to be received.''

Isn't most of our received 'wisdom about animals wrong and all our arguments for using animals post-hoc rationalisations that don't stand up to scrutiny? When have we started seriously looking at animals as they are in themselves rather than how we can use them for our own purposes and using circular reasoning to say our purpose for the animals is their true nature and true purpose?

Experts in Dunning-Kruger

'The Dunning-Kruger effect is a cognitive bias in which people wrongly overestimate their knowledge or ability in a specific area. This tends to occur because a lack of self-awareness prevents them from accurately assessing their own skills.' – (Psychology Today)

For some reason people think vegans will be easy to argue against. Not having studied the issues they make basic philosophical and scientific errors and are overconfident and underprepared. There is also a level of arrogance in the kind unpreparedness displayed by AA Gill in his debate with George Monbiot.
https://www.intelligencesquared.com/events/let-them-eat-meat-theres-nothing-wrong-with-rearing-and-killing-animals-for-human-consumption/
The Great Britain Debate Team debated a team of vegans in the USA. It was a shockingly arrogant display from the British team who seemed to be blissfully unaware of the litany of logical fallacies they were committing. The vegan team came well prepared with facts and figures and efforts to appeal to empathy and fairness. The G.B. team simply avoided engaging on the statistics and used arguments from taste, tradition and personal preference, all delivered with maximum derision and the confidence that can only come from the Dunning-Kruger effect. After the moderator initially called it a draw, it was then decided they won the debate on the deciding factor that they had travelled all the way from the UK!
There's a kind of paradox where you won't know how bad your anti-vegan arguments are until you are vegan and realise how bad your excuses were.
Donald Trump as President of The United States of America was perhaps the best example of the Dunning-Kruger effect in action. It seems the bigger the job the more you can get away with. For actual practical jobs you have to be able to prove competence in more specific parameters and wouldn't get away with bluffing, lies and blatant disregard for facts.

Do Gooder Derogation

One study found that meat eaters asked to list words associated with non-meat eaters listed words like 'arrogant, crazy and annoying'. (1) The study found that this was due to '**anticipated moral reproach**', in other words the participants felt like they were going to be judged by the non-meat eaters so they judged them first. To test this further they further divided the study into participants questioned on whether the non-meat eaters would judge them morally and the negative associations were stronger in the group with more anticipation of this. 'Other research has shown how moral disengagement operates in the deactivation of moral self-regulatory processes when considering the impact of meat consumption. In particular, a 2016 study offered an interpretation of moral disengagement as a motivated reasoning process which is triggered by loss aversion and dissonance avoidance. (2) It will be many vegans experience that you don't actually have to say anything to anyone about veganism for people to become defensive and this is most likely due to their anticipation of judgement and getting theirs in first. The origin of so many arguments about vegans being hypocrites could come from this too. Charges of hypocrisy and moralising are brought up first to defend against the anticipated moral reproach. 'These studies empirically document the backlash reported by moral minorities and trace it back to resentment by the mainstream against feeling morally judged.' (Psychology Today). The study authors identified ways to combat the feeling of being judged from another study on physicians and attitudes to personal fitness. People feeling judged here also responded badly. Two possible strategies were emphasising personal struggles to be more relatable and the more effective strategy emphasized non-judgment of participants. We all make moral judgements and there is no avoiding making a moral evaluation of animal use and slaughter when advocating veganism. People react badly to feeling personally judged.

This feeling of being judged may be at the root of 'getting in first' with thought terminating clichés and trying to limit the scope of morality to a 'personal choice'. 'In follow-up studies, the researchers who studied physician choices examined the effects of two potential strategies physicians could use: 1) admitting to fitness struggles, and 2) emphasizing that their own fitness choices are personal and don't bear on their judgments of others. This brings us back to the reason people find 'personal choice' vegans more palatable than those that include moral judgement.

Morally Motivated Reasoning

Ditto and colleagues likened moral reasoners in everyday situations to lay attorneys than lay judges; people do not reason in the direction from assessment of individual evidence to moral conclusion (bottom-up), but from a preferred moral conclusion to assessment of evidence (top-down). The former resembles the thought process of a judge who is motivated to be accurate, unbiased, and impartial in her decisions; the latter resembles that of an attorney whose goal is to win a dispute using partial and selective arguments (2) Morally motivated reasoning is starting with the conclusion you want and reasoning backwards from there. People start with wanting to consume animal products and build their justifications and distort morality to fit that conclusion. In terms of exploiting and slaughtering animals while claiming to love and care for them it is clear that some mental gymnastics are needed to go from saying you care about animals to sending them to slaughter at the youngest possible age. If people claimed to love dogs but dogs took the place of every animal currently exploited by humans the protestations of love and 'welfare' would be seen for what they are and there would be an outcry. How vegans feel about all animals might be illuminated by imagining if dogs were in all the positions pigs are in and then trying to figure out what the morally relevant difference is between pigs and dogs, meaning one species deserve their fate and the other doesn't. Just one example. Through species overlap the principle can overlap between all species with the morally relevant characteristics, this will be discussed as being sentience later.

What we see is animal slaughter supporters fitting their moral criterion for concern for other animals into the Procrustean bed of their desire for animal products. It just doesn't fit without chopping some limbs off.

Cognitive Dissonance

This is 'the state of having inconsistent thoughts, beliefs, or attitudes, especially as relating to behavioural decisions and attitude change.' (Oxford English Dictionary)

It's important to understand that it is not just holding inconsistent beliefs. The cognitive *dissonance* is best thought of as a lack of harmony, as if one instrument in an orchestra or a section were playing some other tune and creating dissonance rather than the harmony of musical notes together. If this is experienced as some sort of discomfort then the person seeks to resolve the disharmony by making their thoughts, actions, ideas and beliefs align and be more consistent. According to the theory if new information is perceived that clashes with a person's beliefs it may trigger discomfort. To resolve this Leon Festinger proposed that human beings strive for internal psychological consistency. - A Theory of

Cognitive Dissonance (1957). They tend to make changes to justify the stressful behavior, either by adding new parts to the cognition causing the psychological dissonance or by avoiding circumstances and contradictory information likely to increase the magnitude of the cognitive dissonance.

So people can either work to bring their beliefs more in line with the new information or distort or deny that new information to fit in with their previous theories.
Many conspiracy theories, pseudoscience and supernatural beliefs actually accommodate new facts that they simply can't deny by incorporating them into their theory, but they are explained away. Often the way facts are distorted becomes the defining feature of that model. For instance, to explain the reason a prophecy fails a model may incorporate the failed prophecy into itself rather than go with the obvious conclusion that the prophecy was a fraud. Incorporating it could mean that the prophecy was a test and because the true believers passed it then a prophesised calamity never came about. Such models are unfalsifiable and such distortions and assimilations of facts into the models in this way mean they can never be disproven and can continue to exist. Things that should end conspiracies actually serve to shape them and the character of the conspiracy is dictated by the facts they envelope into themselves and the way they are distorted. Inconvenient facts become part of the web of the conspiracy.
Dissonance could be the reason behind sunk cost fallacies where people persist with an action or belief on the rationalisation that they have already put time, effort or other resources into it and so are concerned about wasting those rather than what actually may be a more rational step of abandoning the 'sunk cost' and starting anew.

The important thing to remember is that it's not cognitive

dissonance without the discomfort being felt in some form and the feeling that it needs to be resolved somehow. (3)

'Meat-eating can involve discrepancies between the behavior of eating meat and various ideals that the person holds. (4) Some researchers call this form of moral conflict the *meat paradox*. (5,6) Hank Rothgerber posited that meat eaters may encounter a conflict between their eating behavior and their affections toward animals. This occurs when the dissonant state involves recognition of one's behavior as a meat eater and a belief, attitude, or value that this behavior contradicts. The person with this state may attempt to employ various methods, including avoidance, willful ignorance, dissociation, perceived behavioral change, and do-gooder derogation to prevent this form of dissonance from occurring. Once occurred, he or she may reduce it in the form of motivated cognitions, such as denigrating animals, offering pro-meat justifications, or denying responsibility for eating meat. (4)

Moral disengagement

Moral disengagement is a term from social psychology for the process of convincing the self that ethical standards do not apply to oneself in a particular context. It involves a process of cognitive re-framing of destructive behaviour as being morally acceptable without changing the behaviour or the moral standards. It is a way of rationalising a behaviour through many of the following aspects and they have application in people's arguments for animal use.

- **Moral Justification**

is justifying an action or behaviour as if it has a moral purpose in order to make it socially acceptable. So things that would normally be thought of as unacceptable are given a 'higher purpose'. People arguing like this for animal use will say 'animals are here for us to use' and may employ religious **arguments from authority** to justify animal slaughter. This moral purpose can be 'feeding the world' as most animal 'Agvocates' effuse about even though they are promoting the least efficient model. With these arguments it can be hard to disagree with the general aim, rather it is the unnecessary exploitation and slaughter of animals as a method to achieve the aim that is disputed. Agvocates will try to say that vegans are against farmers or people having freedom to choose and other such general principles, none of which is true. It's an attempt to pass platitudes off as some sort of hokey wisdom that no-one will disagree with except unreasonable vegans of course!

- **Euphemistic labelling**

There are lots of examples of the 'absent referent' as Carol J Adams called other animals and the euphemisms employed to mask animal slaughter.
Carol Adams explains that
'The Sexual Politics of Meat explains the concept of "the absent referent." Behind every meal of meat is an absence: the death of the animal whose place the meat takes. This is the "absent referent." The absent referent functions to cloak the violence inherent to meat eating, to protect the conscience of the meat eater and render the idea of individual animals as immaterial to anyone's selfish desires. It is that which separates the meat eater from the animal and the animal from the end product. The function of the absent referent is to keep our "meat" separated from any idea that she or he was once an animal, to keep something from being seen as having been someone, to allow for the moral abandonment of another being.'

Terms like 'harvesting', 'culling' and even 'euthanasia'

when it doesn't apply are used to refer to slaughtering animals.
The animal flesh and secretions themselves are called names that are distant from the once living, breathing, sentient being.
Individual animals of species are not referred to as individuals but as one homogeneous entity. 'Fish', Sheep' etc – they lose the plural and become one.
It really gets into Orwellian territory when it comes to food labelling. 'Happy Eggs', 'The Laughing Cow' and other labels are jarring when juxtaposed with the reality of the animal's lives and deaths.
The absolute gall of animal exploiters bemoaning vegan food such as Almond MILK being called a MILK when it has been used since Roman times and was a staple in medieval kitchens is astonishing.
Hellmans did an amazing U-Turn going from trying to sue a company for using the term mayonnaise without eggs as an ingredient. (8)(9)
The argument from such protectionism of food terms is that consumers will be confused by plant based alternatives. Are you confused by the existence of these alternatives?
Suicide Food documented how animals are depicted wanting to willingly sacrifice themselves to be consumed by humans in some sort of perverse Stockholm Syndrome where Douglas Adam's thought experiment becomes a reality. (10)

- **Advantageous Comparison**

'individuals contrast their conduct with other examples of more immoral behavior and in doing this comparison their own behavior is trivialized. The more immoral the contrasting behavior is, the more likely it is that one's destructive behavior will seem less bad. These so-called exonerating comparisons rely on the moral justification by utilitarian standards. Two sets of judgements facilitate making destructive behavior morally acceptable.'

The fallacy of relative privation, whataboutism and 'not as bad as' arguments have their origin here in this attempt at moral justification. It's ultimately an immature response to a harm being pointed out. It's been speculated that so many arguments against veganism are at this sort of inchoate infantile level because people haven't thought through these arguments since the time they were taught it was acceptable to exploit and slaughter animals. A curious child may ask why we eat animals and their questions will be brushed off and dismissed with the fallacious arguments and bucolic myths of how that's just the way things are and that it is normal and necessary and that's what those animal's purpose is. We usually learn that 'two wrongs don't make a right' at this youthful stage of our lives too but exceptions are made when it comes to animal use to gratify our tastes. Being indoctrinated in the myths of animal use at such a young age, most people don't give a second thought to the issues until they encounter a vegan arguing against them. It's then that they reach back in time to bring forth the only arguments they have at their disposal, those myths they were taught in youth and have never challenged since. If you are offended by this, just think how many anti-vegan arguments are of this nature, all the 'you too', 'but I like it', but everyone else does it', 'but a vegan was mean to me' are of this childish nature.

Displacement of responsibility, operates by distorting the relationship between actions and the effects they cause. People behave in ways they would normally oppose if a legitimate authority accepts responsibility for the consequences of that behavior.' Authorities and organizations are seen as the morally responsible agents and so the individual displaces their responsibility for their actions onto these authorities.

This is seen in people saying they aren't personally responsible for slicing animal's throats or grinding up day old chicks alive in macerators. The responsibility is placed on slaughterhouse workers and the companies that exploit and slaughter animals.

While these corporations that profit from animal use are reprehensible it does not mean individuals are not responsible for their actions. They still hold certain harmful attitudes and prejudices towards other animals and seek to justify animal exploitation and commodification.

For more on this subject I recommend
https://nationalpost.com/news/politics/so-you-think-corporations-are-responsible-for-the-worlds-emissions-its-not-that-simple

- **Diffusion of Responsibility**

The appeal to popularity fallacy often appears here. The diffusion of responsibility is where people say everybody else is doing something so it is therefore justified.

Diffusion of responsibility occurs in a group of people, where with the increasing number of people, the level of diffusion increases. In this phenomenon, a person has lower inclination towards responsibility as they feel that others are also equally responsible in the group. Assumptions are made on the basis that other people are responsible for taking action. Responsibility is diffused by division of labor. Tasks that are subdivided seem harmless and easy to carry out. This shifts attention to the details of their specific job. Decision making in groups is a practice that makes otherwise polite people to behave inhumanely. Collective action provides anonymity, which allows weakening of moral control. Any harmful activity carried out in the group can be associated to others actions. People in groups act inhumanely when they [are not] personally held accountable for their actions

- **Disregarding or misrepresenting injurious consequences**

This manifests as denial of the harms of animal exploitation. Animals are not seen or regarded as victims of exploitation and slaughter. It is hard to think of a more blatant denialism than that of the harms of animal agriculture which confines and slaughters trillions of individuals annually.

- **Dehumanisation**

What is labelled dehumanisation here applies to how humans are seen as less than human in order to justify their exploitation and slaughter and otherwise horrendous treatment. This becomes a sticking point for many when we talk about other animals in this context as the dehumanisation has meant 'humans are treated like animals' – what is analogous here is that animals are treated like animals. In fact it is the de-animalisation of animals that happens – they are thought of as commodities and objects rather than sentient individuals with their own interests.

Desentientisation – the denial of mind to animals used. (11) From the article 'Many people like eating meat, but most are reluctant to harm things that have minds. The current three studies show that this dissonance motivates people to deny minds to animals. Study 1 demonstrates that animals considered appropriate for human consumption are ascribed diminished mental capacities. Study 2 shows that meat eaters are motivated to deny minds to food animals when they are reminded of the link between meat and animal suffering. Finally, Study 3 provides direct support for our dissonance hypothesis, showing that expectations regarding the immediate consumption of meat increase mind denial. Moreover, this mind denial in turn reduces negative affect associated with dissonance. The findings highlight the role of dissonance reduction in facilitating the practice of meat eating and protecting cultural commitments.' (12)

Meat paradox

According to psychologists Brock Bastian and Steve Loughnan, (13) who do research on the topic in Australia, the "meat paradox" is the "psychological conflict between people's dietary preference for meat and their moral response to animal suffering". They argue that "bringing harm to others is inconsistent with a view of oneself as a moral person. As such, meat consumption leads to negative effects for meat-eaters because they are confronted with a view of themselves that is unfavourable: how can I be a good person and also eat meat?" (14)

Perceptions of animals exploited for food.

'Ethical conflicts arise when eating animals if they are considered to have moral status. Perceptions of animals' moral status vary greatly, but are determined in part by perceptions of animals as having conscious minds and able to experience pain, and their perceived similarity to humans. Some social psychologists hypothesize that meat eaters can reduce discomfort associated with the meat paradox by minimizing their perception of these morally

relevant qualities in animals, particularly animals they regard as food, and several recent studies provide support for this hypothesis. It was found, for instance, that by simply being classified within the food animals group, an animal is immediately attributed fewer moral rights.
A series of studies published in 2015 asked meat-eating American and Australian undergraduates to "list three reasons why you think it is OK to eat meat." Over 90% of participants offered reasons which the researchers classified among the "four N's":

- Appeals to human evolution or to carnivory in nature ("natural")
- Appeals to societal or historical norms ("normal")
- Appeals to nutritive or environmental necessity ("necessary")
- Appeals to the tastiness of meat ("nice")

The researchers found that these justifications were effective in reducing moral tension associated with the meat paradox.' (15)

Here we have the phenomenon where the desired outcome of wanting to consume animals means that morally motivated reasoning is employed. All the areas we have covered so far come into play to 'resolve' this 'meat paradox' – any cognitive dissonance is alleviated, all the rationalisations are employed to engage in a sort of victim blaming where instead of simply acknowledging that animals can be victims and adapting their behaviour to avoid animal use, they maintain the desire for animal use through post hoc rationalisations which include diminishing the moral status of animals.

It's been shown that merely labelling animals as destined for a certain purpose means they are viewed to have less moral status. This is disastrous for many millions of individuals of certain species. Rather than see animals as they are, we assign them lesser value as a way to make ourselves feel less guilty about exploiting and slaughtering them.

What is needed is a fundamental shift in how we view other animals. We can't begin to see them clearly when we are employing all these rationalisations after the fact of wanting to consume them. (16)

"We need another and a wiser and perhaps a more mystical concept of animals. Remote from universal nature and living by complicated artifice, man in civilization surveys the creature through the glass of his knowledge and sees thereby a feather magnified and the whole image in distortion. We patronize them for their incompleteness, for their tragic fate for having taken form so far below ourselves. And therein do we err. For the animal shall not be measured by man. In a world older and more complete than ours, they move finished and complete, gifted with the extension of the senses we have lost or never attained, living by voices we shall never hear. They are not brethren, they are not underlings: they are other nations, caught with ourselves in the net of life and time, fellow prisoners of the splendour and travail of the earth."

— Henry Beston, *The Outermost House: A Year of Life on the Great Beach of Cape Cod*

Customary farming exemptions

The different attitudes to animals has resulted in some bizarre exemptions through history. A ban on eating mammals during Lent saw Catholics reclassify two species of mammals as fish. As Scientific American reports *'in the 17th century, the Bishop of Quebec approached his superiors in the Church and asked whether his flock would*

be permitted to eat beaver meat on Fridays during Lent, despite the fact that meat-eating was forbidden. Since the semi-aquatic rodent was a skilled swimmer, the Church declared that the beaver was a fish. Being a fish, beaver barbeques were permitted throughout Lent. Problem solved!
The Church, by the way, also classified another semi-aquatic rodent, the capybara, as a fish for dietary purposes. The critter, the largest rodent in the world, is commonly eaten during Lent in Venezuela.'

This Gerrymandering of the supposed morally relevant distinctions between species that humans want to consume leads to absurd results like the Catholic Church's declarations, but modern farming practices are no different in the absurd lines they draw. The Moral Gerrymandering of 'Customary Farming Exemptions' means that what would be considered cruel if done to a dog or a cat is standard practice in animal agriculture. The law against cruelty to animals has to be ignored when it comes to certain species in order for animal farming to be able to exist. Could animal agriculture exist without bestiality or cruelty being made exception for?
If one rabbit is labelled as a 'food animal' and another as a 'wild animal' or 'pet' why would doing the same things to one but not the other land you with a criminal record and probably an FBI file as a potential serial killer? The case of a man who was charged with cruelty for running a lawnmower over some ducklings while people can grind chicks alive in egg production highlights this disparity and Gerrymandering. (17)
Rabbits are classified as 'poultry' by the USDA. This is not due to any objective scientific categorisation or an assessment of moral status that seeks to be as fair as possible to an animal's interests and nature. Rather it is a classification designed to serve the animal exploitation

industries so that they can slaughter the animals with fewer restrictions.

Compartmentalisation

Compartmentalization is a subconscious psychological defense mechanism used to avoid cognitive dissonance, or the mental discomfort and anxiety caused by a person's having conflicting values and beliefs within themselves. It is analogous to fencing of or boxing away a certain area so that it is not subject to the same standards or criticism as other areas, or so that cognitive dissonance is not felt.

Just as with the Dunning-Kruger effect, someone can be a genius in one area of study but not realise their limitations and lack of knowledge in others.

I think we need both science and philosophy. Philosophers can make very naïve scientific errors and scientists can commit basic logical fallacies and lack philosophical insights. The two can act as checks and balances on each other, although of course as far as science goes it is the best self-correcting method we have and it tries to eliminate any biases and arrive at more accurate models.

Few subjects can expose the naiveté that experts in one field can have in another like veganism can.
Scientists like Neil DeGrasse Tyson are excellent educators in their areas of expertise. The confidence they feel in holding forth on any subject asked of them extends to veganism when they are asked about breeding animals in relation to climate change in Q&A sessions and leads to astoundingly vacuous answers. Tyson was asked such a question and his answers revealed glib musings that were the opposite of the facts on the subject. (18) Tyson employed numerous fallacies and was under the impression

that local food is better as transport accounts for a larger share of GHG gas emissions than food choice. In fact, Weber and Matthews found that although "food miles" contribute to the carbon footprint, an average of 83% of a food product's carbon footprint is caused during production. Transportation accounts for only 11% of the product's greenhouse gas emissions. So the positive impact of switching to a vegan diet is many times greater than that of "buying local".

Tyson could be forgiven for not knowing the facts if he wasn't the first to pick up on the grievous errors of others and wasn't in a position of massive influence. As a science educator it behooves him to be well informed and if he isn't then he should withhold spreading misinformation from his platforms. He should be aware of personal prejudice possibly affecting his judgement on the subject and be cautious in areas where he is not an expert. The idea of the localness of a food's origin being the most important variable seems to be an intuitive misconception. As Hannah Ritchie writes in 'You want to reduce the carbon footprint of your food? Focus on what you eat, not whether your food is local'

'Transport is a small contributor to emissions. For most food products, it accounts for less than 10%, and it's much smaller for the largest GHG emitters. In beef from beef herds, it's 0.5%. Not just transport, but all processes in the supply chain after the food left the farm – processing, transport, retail and packaging – mostly account for a small share of emissions. This data shows that this is the case when we look at individual food products. But studies also shows that this holds true for actual diets; here we show the results of a study which looked at the footprint of diets across the EU. Food transport was responsible for only 6% of emissions, whilst dairy, meat and eggs accounted for 83%.

Whether you buy it from the farmer next door or from far away, it is not the location that makes the carbon footprint of your dinner large, but the fact that it is beef.' (19)

Tyson also says that it is what they are bred for and the animals wouldn't exist in nature otherwise. He also mistakes making descriptive arguments with making prescriptive judgements about what we should do. If dogs are bred solely for the purpose of fighting does that make it justified?

Many scientists and engineers will naturally seek technological solutions to humanity's problems and in the case of feeding large populations it is no different. Tyson proposes that technology may be able to 'scrub' CO_2 from the air and provide a technological fix to climate change. This is an example of the 'distancing' we discussed – deferring solutions to an unknown future date rather than taking advantage of the already available best options. In one sense there is nothing wrong with seeking new technological solutions but many are unproven at this stage. (20) We are also time limited in the window of opportunity to apply the best current solutions. Without addressing the impact of meat of dairy on the environment scientists are warning that meeting climate targets as set out in the Paris Climate Agreement will be unachievable. Even if all other areas of greenhouse gas emissions were addressed in a best case scenario a failure to address animal agriculture always pushes us over planetary boundaries and the limits set. (21)

It's interesting how the idea of technological fixes is used differently depending on the person's ideology. If they are vegan they will see technology as a good way to feed humans directly and further improve the efficiency and reduce the impact of plant agriculture. However for those clinging on to an ideology of animal use who can't see beyond that paradigm they think of using the technology or innovations to try and improve how animals are fed to try and make feed conversion ratios a little more ecologically efficient. So farms are used for animal feed, masks are worn by cows to capture their methane emissions and cows wear virtual reality helmets to keep them calm. These absurdities can only arise from trying to find loopholes in a flawed system.

Can we ever expect to see a retraction of these statements from DeGrasse Tyson and promotion of the facts in their place? For a science educator to be repeating these memes is highly unfortunate but probably goes unnoticed by the majority, especially when there is a credulous audience who want their prejudices confirmed.

Noam Chomsky is consistently placed in top ten charts of public intellectuals but seemed irritated by questions about veganism and responds curtly about rights and responsibilities in order to justify animal slaughter. On one occasion he immediately turns around a perfectly reasonable question onto his interlocutor to ask about where we draw the line and do they kill mosquitoes? – a **continuum fallacy** and a question that he would know the answer to if he had ever read Tom Regan. (If he has, he has failed to assimilate the logical answer.) He also employs a fallacy of relative privation, slippery slope fallacy and continuum fallacy saying that if we examine things that we might support that are immoral it takes too much time to examine everything and we should prioritise human affairs. This is Chomsky's version of 'there's no ethical consumption under capitalism' so therefore support animal exploitation and slaughter. He also ignores the many ways animal agriculture is a major contributor to major threats to human life and wreaks havoc on the natural world. (22)

Naturalist and broadcaster David Attenborough has in recent years given overtures to the idea that meat and dairy consumption needs to be reduced for the sake of the natural world. However, when asked directly about his personal attitude to animals he remarks that he is not an animal lover.

Q. – ''When you see that sort of intelligence in animals, doesn't that make you want to be vegetarian?''
A- ''No. If you understand about the natural world, we're a part of the system and you can't feed lions grass. But because we have the intelligence to choose… But we haven't got the gut to allow us to be totally vegetarian for a start. You can tell by the shape of our guts and the shape of our teeth that we evolved to be omnivores. We aren't carnivores like lions but neither are we elephants.''

Sir David's response is bizarre to say the least. Who is suggesting feeding lions grass? He then says we have the capacity for choice as moral agents but seems to stop himself continuing this line of thought as it may lead to making the choice to eat grass. His remark about guts is not supported by science. (23) He appeals to the fact we have the teeth of omnivores and makes the leap from this observation to say it determines what we should eat.

So his answer is based mainly around a biological determinism which he thinks obligates us to consume animals. (24) Perhaps he has started to change his mind as he has more recently made statements about the need to reduce meat consumption, albeit for purely environmental reasons it appears.

Brian Cox may be an affable science communicator but he is literally a bacon troll.

Professor Brian Cox @ProfBrianCox Mar 24, 2013
'If I get more than 10 tweets from vegetarians I will cook an extra steak just for fun. #shutupandsaveacow'

It seems it is too much to expect even a modicum of maturity when the subject of using and slaughtering animals arises, even from renowned scientists and highly intelligent people.

Compare and contrast this with this post from Brian Greene, an equally brilliant science communicator, but one who is vegan.

Professor Brian Greene @bgreene
'Yup....And if we all went vegan, we'd go a long way toward dealing with climate change while also boosting overall health.'

This Tweet is met with outrage and comments about how Brian should 'stick to physics'. It's remarkable people don't realise this *is* physics! As Brian explains in 'The Fabric of the Cosmos' - 'If we follow the food chain, we ultimately come upon animals (like me) that eat only plants. How do plants and their products of fruit and vegetables maintain low entropy? Through photosynthesis, plants use sunlight to separate ambient carbon dioxide into oxygen, which is given back to the environment, and carbon, which the plants use to grow and flourish. So we can trace the low entropy non-animal sources of energy back to the sun'. Ultimately, entropy is relevant if we are examining ecological efficiency and the Second law of Thermodynamics. Eating lower of the food chain is closer to the low entropy state of higher order and more efficient!

Philosopher and logician Bertrand Russell once remarked of vegetarians that, "if they refuse to eat meat because of

humanitarian principles, they should also refuse to eat bread," i.e. because we have to kill wheat in order to make it. (Harris 1972, 108) - Harris, John. 1972. 'Killing for Food'.
He also stated, "The fact that an opinion has been widely held is no evidence that it is not utterly absurd; indeed, in view of the silliness of the majority of mankind, a widespread belief is more often likely to be foolish than sensible. There is no impersonal reason for regarding the interests of human beings as more important than those of animals. We can destroy animals more easily than they can destroy us; that is the only solid basis of our claim to superiority."

The contradiction here may arise from the difference of theorising about animal interests and then having to actually put it into practice in your life, resulting in the 'plants tho' gambit that is greedy reductionism and unscientific.

The very nature of human knowledge means we can have a good general knowledge but as we specialise and gain deeper knowledge in one subject it is more focussed in a narrower area. Rather than admitting our ignorance in some areas we pretend to be able to extrapolate our expertise to other areas we actually know little about. This is the case with the aforementioned experts who display beginner level knowledge when it comes to vegan issues. We can speculate on their own psychological reasons for this and unresolved cognitive dissonance they may have. The fact remains that they would be the first to 'call out' others spreading disinformation of this sort, especially on evolution or climate change which tend to attract more denialism because it affects people's sense of self and personal habits in ways other sciences do not. The same is true for veganism which challenges human supremacy, speciesism and sense of self directly. The most controversial scientific theories have this in common, usually decentring humanity whether Earth is put in its rightful place challenging the geocentric model with the Copernican revolution or decentring humans through the realisation that we are one species among millions that have evolved through natural selection on Earth. Freud claimed his theories were the third great such revolution that showed we weren't psychologically centred. At a time when there is a climate crisis and a zoonotic pandemic the pandering to animal exploiters is cowardly and a real disservice to humanity and the animals we share Earth with. At a time when radical action is needed most communicators and educators add caveats to the end of every article saying they don't expect people to actually go vegan.

Why not?

Probably because they haven't done so themselves. This weak messaging usually comes after an article explains how dire the situation is and the damage that animal agriculture does. They just can't help themselves though, it's as if they are projecting their own moral cowardice onto the public at large. They have to ameliorate the message to keep the audience happy – but when did these 'fearless truth tellers' become so timid in telling the truth? This is the trouble with affable nice guy figures communicating that 'you don't have to be vegan'. People think if they are nice but support eating baby animals it must be okay then. Similarly scientists not taking a leadership role with regards to changing diets during the largest loss of biodiversity, slaughter of animals and the ongoing climate crisis should be a source of embarrassment amongst critical thinkers.

It's clear that people like this who think veganism is extreme have not comprehended even a small percentage of the magnitude of animal exploitation and slaughter and the existential crisis that threatens humanity.

Veganism is seen as extreme in proportion to how normalised violence against other animals is.

If we contrast the supposed extremism of avoiding all forms of animal use and slaughter with the myriad ways in which animals are exploited and slaughtered which do you honestly think is the more extreme action? You have just been conditioned to see abstaining from violence to animals as extreme because the violence is socially acceptable and ubiquitous.

On a scale of zero to global zoonotic pandemic caused by eating animals, how extreme do you think veganism is?

Many of the public intellectual figures will display some or all of the following when it comes to veganism.
They will come up with more sophisticated excuses like relative privation or a utilitarian calculus.
They might pay **lip service** to the idea of veganism or some future adoption of plant based diets or technological alternatives to animal use but not take the best currently available options. Richard Dawkins, Noam Chomsky and Bill Nye all speculate that society will shift more towards adoption of plant-based diets in the future, possibly through necessity.
They know the facts but display **slothful induction** in not putting them together and being vegan.

"Humans — who enslave, castrate, experiment on, and fillet other animals — have had an understandable penchant for pretending animals do not feel pain. A sharp distinction between humans and 'animals' is essential if we are to bend them to our will, make them work for us, wear them, eat them — without any disquieting tinges of guilt or regret. It is unseemly of us, who often behave so unfeelingly toward other animals, to contend that only humans can suffer. The behavior of other animals renders such pretensions specious. They are just too much like us."

- Carl Sagan

Confirmation Bias

'Still a man hears what he wants to hear
And disregards the rest' – Paul Simon

I think this is most often seen when vegans are accused of propaganda and people ignore the billions spent by companies lobbying for meat and dairy, the massive disparity in subsidies for those compared to fruit and vegetables and the amount of vegan advertising compared to the amount of adverts for animal products.

I think these cognitive biases and psychological factors represents greater barriers to the adoption of veganism than any actual logical arguments.

Recommended Reading

Why People Hate Vegans -
https://www.theguardian.com/lifeandstyle/2019/oct/25/why-do-people-hate-vegans

The Hidden Biases That Drive Anti-Vegan Hatred -
https://www.bbc.com/future/article/20200203-the-hidden-biases-that-drive-anti-vegan-hatred

Vegan Killjoys at the Table—Contesting Happiness and Negotiating Relationships with Food Practices -
https://ideas.repec.org/a/gam/jsoctx/v4y2014i4p623-639d41999.html

Why Vegans Make Some People So Uncomfortable and Angry -
https://www.psychologytoday.com/gb/blog/without-prejudice/201910/why-vegans-make-some-people-so-uncomfortable-and-angry

Why Some People Resent Do-Gooders -
https://www.psychologytoday.com/gb/blog/in-love-and-war/201706/why-some-people-resent-do-gooders

Notes to Chapter Three

(1) https://faculty.wharton.upenn.edu/wp-content/uploads/2011/12/Minson---Monin,-2011.pdf
(2) http://sites.uci.edu/peterdittolab/files/2015/03/Ditto-et-al-MMR-Chapter.pdf
(3) Thanks to Phoenix from the PhoenixRising87 YouTube channel for teaching me this along with the name for the fallacy of relative privation featured later in the book.
(4) Rothgerber, Hank (2020). "Meat-related cognitive dissonance: A conceptual framework for understanding how meat eaters reduce negative arousal from eating animals". Appetite. Elsevier.
(5) Loughnan, Steve; Bastian, Brock; Haslam, Nick (2014). "The Psychology of Eating Animals". Current Directions in Psychological Science. Sage Journals. 23 (2): 104–108.
(6) Bastian, Brock; Loughnan, Steve (2016). "Resolving the Meat-Paradox: A Motivational Account of Morally Troublesome Behavior and Its Maintenance" (PDF). Personality and Social Psychology Review. Sage Journals. 21 (3): 278–299.
(7) https://www.atlasobscura.com/articles/almond-milk-obsession-origins-middle-ages
(8) https://www.bbc.co.uk/news/business-30004158
(9) https://metro.co.uk/2016/02/03/hellmanns-launches-vegan-mayo-after-trying-to-sue-eggless-spread-rival-5660516/
(10) http://suicidefood.blogspot.com/
(11) https://www.sciencedirect.com/science/article/abs/pii/S0195666317318846
(12) https://journals.sagepub.com/doi/abs/10.1177/0146167211424291
(13) https://www.sciencedirect.com/science/article/abs/pii/S0195666317318846#:~:text=Specifically%2C%20the%20meat%20paradox%20describes,dissonance%20which%20elicits%20aversive%20arousal.
(14) – BBC FUTURE https://www.bbc.com/future/article/20190206-what-the-meat-paradox-reveals-about-moral-decision-making.
(15) https://en.wikipedia.org/wiki/Psychology_of_eating_meat
(16) https://theconversation.com/the-meat-paradox-how-we-can-love-some-animals-and-eat-others-149
(17) See - https://people.com/celebrity/man-runs-over-ducklings-with-lawn-mower-sentenced-to-year-in-jail/
(18) Neil DeGrasse Tyson response to question in plant-based diets - https://www.youtube.com/watch?v=In6YtNK9PCs
(19) Local versus Vegan resources

You want to reduce the carbon footprint of your food? Focus on what you eat, not whether your food is local by Hannah Ritchie
https://ourworldindata.org/food-choice-vs-eating-local
Food-Miles and the Relative Climate Impacts of Food Choices in the United States - Christopher L. Weber* and H. Scott Matthews - https://pubs.acs.org/doi/full/10.1021/es702969f
Do food miles really matter? -https://green.harvard.edu/news/do-food-miles-really-matter
Locally Grown Produce - https://skeptoid.com/episodes/4162
Carnegie Mellon Researchers Report Dietary Choice Has Greater Impact on Climate Change Than Food Miles - https://www.cmu.edu/news/archive/2008/April/april17_foodmiles.shtml
(20) Technology - https://www.sciencedaily.com/releases/2020/04/200420125510.htm
(21) https://www.carbonbrief.org/meat-and-dairy-consumption-could-mean-a-two-degree-target-is-off-the-table
https://www.theguardian.com/environment/2018/oct/10/huge-reduction-in-meat-eating-essential-to-avoid-climate-breakdown
https://www.independent.co.uk/environment/meat-climate-change-paris-agreement-vegetarian-b1621033.html
(22) As I write Catherine Klein has started a series of videos about famous skeptic's comments on veganism which is well worth checking out to see the absurd arguments they use and the corners they paint themselves into. See Sam Harris and Richard Dawkins who are covered so far.
Harris - https://www.youtube.com/watch?v=QloaW-hBiTg&t=871s
Dawkins - https://www.youtube.com/watch?v=6ZO5_WjOG-c
Noam Chomsky's comments can be found in this Seb Alex video - https://www.youtube.com/watch?v=f7-E4cKtL5s
Chomsky on Animal Rights
http://generic.wordpress.soton.ac.uk/skywritings/2019/01/01/noam-chomsky-on-animals-and-responsibilities/
(23) see for example - https://translational-medicine.biomedcentral.com/articles/10.1186/s12967-017-1175-y
(24) David Attenborough - https://metro.co.uk/2013/01/29/david-attenborough-im-not-an-animal-lover-3370670/?ito=cbshare

Chapter Four

Facts and Fallacies

Critical Thinking

'What skeptical thinking boils down to is the means to construct, and to understand, a reasoned argument and—especially important—to recognize a fallacious or fraudulent argument. The question is not whether we like the conclusion that emerges out of a train of reasoning, but whether the conclusion follows from the premise or starting point and whether that premise is true.'

'In addition to teaching us what to do when evaluating a claim to knowledge, any good baloney detection kit must also teach us what not to do. It helps us recognize the most common and perilous fallacies of logic and rhetoric. Many good examples can be found in religion and politics, because their practitioners are so often obliged to justify two contradictory propositions.'

- **Carl Sagan** (1)

"There are three good reasons to avoid logical fallacies in your writing. First, logical fallacies are wrong and, simply put, dishonest if you use them knowingly. Second, they take away from the strength of your argument. Finally, the use of logical fallacies can make your readers feel that you do not consider them to be very intelligent."

- William R. Smalzer (2)

A logical fallacy is an error in reasoning that renders an argument invalid. There are formal fallacies which come from the structure, hence 'form', of the argument. These are found in deductive arguments. The fallacy can be determined from analysis of the structure of the argument itself. Informal fallacies are every other type of argument that is invalid because the conclusion does not follow from the premises but not due to the form of the argument. These come from inductive arguments. From this we can see that almost any invalid argument can be an informal fallacy but there are common types and so they are categorised. We will look at some of the most common fallacies you will come across when people argue against veganism. I will also detail some that vegans should avoid and that they may be susceptible to.

It should be noted that a fallacy only occurs if someone is attempting to make an argument. If they are building a case for the use and slaughter of other animals and they state that things have always been done this way for millennia and so it should continue we can see that this is their reason for it to continue with the premise being 'it has been done for a long time' and the conclusion that they are claiming follows from this is 'so animal slaughter should continue'. Most fallacies are non sequiturs where the conclusion does not follow from the premise. In this case does the fact something has been done for a long time mean it has to continue, even if it is proven to be harmful or that there are better alternatives? Once we are sure that the claim they are making is indeed their argument then we can confidently identify any possible fallacies. That doesn't always mean telling the person they are using a fallacy. This may or may not be useful in vegan advocacy and debates. It's always

useful to know it yourself so you know what their argument is. However a Socratic Method of questioning may prove better for advocacy.
If someone is merely stating an opinion it is not fallacy unless they are attempting to prove some conclusion logically follows from their statement.

So we can be mistaken in identifying fallacies, it's not always useful and then there is even an infinite regression of 'fallacy fallacies'! This is where someone says a conclusion is wrong because a fallacy has been used. In fact the conclusion may be correct but the means used to reach it is invalid. But just because someone has used the fallacy fallacy doesn't mean their conclusion is wrong…! People also mistakenly think they are using arguments that might be subject to fallacious or sound reasoning when they aren't.
Oftentimes people merely state their opinion or taste as if they are making an argument. They aren't providing a premise and conclusion or any logical structure.

'What can be stated without proof can be dismissed without proof' – Christopher Hitchens.

These type of statements are often descriptive but not prescriptive. Merely observing that animals eat other animals is just a descriptive argument. Once someone says 'animals eat other animals therefore humans should eat other animals' then it's game on. We have an argument and a claim being made now. So always look for whether a claim is being made and ask for clarification of what they are claiming. This can often in itself be enough to make them realise they are just making an observation and not making a case for anything. Observations are just statements of fact, a prescriptive argument on the other hand makes a case for what we should do. Look for keywords 'ought to' and 'should' as signs that a statement is prescriptive and is making a case for what we should do. Merely observing what people already do is descriptive. If you find yourself wondering what point someone is trying to make it is probably due to the fact that they are just being descriptive of how things are and not saying how they should or could be.

It is vital to be aware of these invalid arguments so we can detect them and, just as crucially, avoid them ourselves to build stronger arguments.

The fallacy of relative privation.

'Relative' means in comparison to something else, not absolute – 'privation' means loss or absence of a quality or attribute that would normally be present - 'Relative privation' means losing the quality of being an issue due to comparison to something else.
This is a common fallacy that is encountered when vegan arguments are presented. It takes the form of saying things could be worse or things could be better and using that to reason against the position presented. It is an invalid argument because the relative comparison does not mean the thing initially presented is rendered not good or bad in its own right.

An example would be the common form of the argument that 'there are worse things going on in the world' used as a reason to dismiss advocating for animal rights. (3)

If we think about it in other contexts we can see what the fallacy is. If someone says they have broken a bone and someone says it is not as bad as an earthquake which kills hundreds we can see that they are using the worse problem as an argument to dismiss the present problem. It becomes a fallacy when used as an argument to dismiss problems. Prioritising issues doesn't necessarily mean the fallacy is being used. For example the NHS has an Atlas of Risks which shows the most likely causes of death.

In advocacy for issues around justice this fallacy will be used by those who want to maintain the status quo and are upset by any advocacy for change. It can be reactionary in this way and any issue that someone dislikes is dismissed as 'not as important' as other things going on in the world.

It's a good example of arguments that are selectively used against veganism and animal rights and aren't brought up in the same way against areas the person might support. A good test of an argument is often whether it is only ever brought up against veganism or is used independently and pro-actively on its own terms.

You don't use your anti-vegan arguments against the areas of animal use you already oppose.

However, when it's convenient to do so people will bring up 'worse' problems in the world. It's designed to invalidate the highlighting of a current issue. The problem may in fact not be as bad as other problems. This is going to be true for every problem that isn't deemed the absolute worst in the world at that time. Such a hierarchy can be used to say anything is 'not as bad as' the very worst problem. Doing so does not mean the original problem is not in fact an issue in its own right. If your car breaks down and someone says 'there are worse things in the world' or 'your car could have exploded and killed you' that doesn't mean your car is not broken down and in need of repair.

The same holds true in an animal rights context. It is debateable that there are larger and more pressing issues that the greatest systemic exploitation and slaughter of trillions of animals a year. The climate change, loss of biodiversity, pollution and antibiotic resistance as well as potential for zoonotic pandemics, cost to public health are large issues of a magnitude it is hard to match. 'Poor air quality is the largest environmental health risk in the United States and worldwide, and agriculture is a major source of air pollution. Nevertheless, air quality has been largely absent from discussions about the health and environmental impacts of food. We estimate the air quality–related health impacts of agriculture in the United States, finding that 80% of the 15,900 annual deaths that result from food-related fine particulate matter (PM2.5) pollution are attributable to animal-based foods.' (4)
Aside from the debate on the relative position of issues, the fact remains that using relative privation to reason against an issue is a fallacy. (5) If relative privation is an attempt at invalidation through relative comparisons then the Nirvana fallacy is a similar attempt but due to comparison to an idealised solution.
In this game only the highest priority most absolutely important issue should be dealt with and all time and resources spent on solving that problem. Otherwise someone can always say there is something bigger to worry about.

It also doesn't mean not prioritising where necessary. The fallacy is in the use of the argument to attempt to invalidate other problems. Just because a heart operation is more important than a tooth extraction doesn't mean the toothache is of no importance.

It's also not necessarily true depending on what we are talking about. Any risk atlas is going to put climate change, antibiotic resistance, zoonotic pandemics, food waste, species extinction, biodiversity loss, pollution and the sheer scale of animal exploitation and suffering as bigger issues on a global scale and as an existential threat than anything else.

When people are criticising vegans haven't they got bigger issues to worry about themselves rather than criticising vegans at that point in time? They often end up spending more time subsequently arguing with the vegan who may just have stated one or two facts in a concise manner.

We can also apply our test of whether this is something people say on dog rescue sites. If the species changes to a farmed animal then all of a sudden the same time and effort that would be acceptable to use to save a dog and praise such actions becomes subject to this fallacy.

We can see here the demonstration of how the fallacy occurs when there is a rejection of the importance of our point due to something else's importance. It is a failure to demonstrate that the original point has zero importance and quite often we aren't making any hierarchical claims as to relative importance.

Whataboutisms

'Whataboutisms' are the technique or practice of responding to an accusation or difficult question by making a counter-accusation or raising a different issue.
Again, it isn't invalid to merely observe other issues and problems in the world. What we must ask is about their relevance and what bearing it has on our argument.
These arguments take an easily identifiable form that gives the fallacy its name
What about…
 …plants tho?
…harvest deaths?
…slave labour?
What would make a 'whataboutism' argument valid?
It's not that the issue being raised is not worthy of consideration or is indeed not a problem in itself. Rather it is the attempt to dismiss the vegan argument through the existence of other issues. There may be some crossover with the areas covered by veganism in the whataboutism and it may be a valid area of concern. In examining the harvest deaths argument we will see the different ways these arguments can be employed and whether this is in good faith. This is covered in the chapter on reflexive arguments.
What makes a whataboutism fallacious is when it is used as a variation of the Tu quoque fallacy.
Whataboutisms were particularly associated with Soviet-era Russian propaganda. Any criticism of Russian Gulags, policies, imprisonment of dissidents, censorship etc was met with 'what about…' and then turning it around on some immoral act of The West. The technique functions as a diversionary tactic to distract the opponent from their

original criticism. The technique is used to avoid directly refuting or disproving the opponent's initial argument. The tactic is an attempt at moral relativism, and a form of false moral equivalence. It is considered a form of Tu quoque which is a logical fallacy, because whether or not the original accuser is likewise guilty of an offense has no bearing on the truth value of the original accusation.
(Merriam Webster)

Whataboutisms can lead to the next type of fallacy known as the Nirvana fallacy. Also known as a 'perfect solution fallacy' it may be employed after arguing how many other problems there are in the world and crop up if it's being pointed out that your proposed solution can't solve all the problems. The fallacy occurs if it is argued that a proposed solution or part-solution should be rejected because it does not compare favourably with an idealised solution (the 'Nirvana' of the fallacy's name). As we can always compare anything anyone proposes with a perfect solution and it will fall short it can be a type of appeal to futility. Unless a solution is perfect then it is not worth trying. These type of critics of veganism don't actually want to look at practical solutions to the issues they raise. If they did then the issues wouldn't solely be raised by them in the context of mentioning veganism and to criticise vegans. We would see the campaigning and advocating on these issues in their own right and offering practical solutions. What we actually see is these sort of criticisms become viral Tweets that get thousands of shares and likes from a credulous audience eager to hear bad things about veganism. When these critics bring up issues like animals being killed by harvest machinery and farm worker's rights it isn't because they care about finding solutions to those issues. Often when asked about crop deaths they'll say they don't care, but vegans should. In fact they would be fine if vegans didn't care because then it creates the moral equivalence and no-one has to care about any of the issues. This is the real aim of these arguments. To create such confusion and despair that everyone just throws their hands up and becomes apathetic. No one can then advocate for anything and we are back to the purpose behind the thought terminating clichés and wanting to take morality off the table and making everything a morally equivalent 'personal choice'.

Do vegans use 'whataboutisms'? If they do say 'what about… other animals?' it is used to extend concern to more areas of animal use and to more animals. It is not used to dismiss the original area of animal use that was being highlighted and that's the difference. Vegans don't support that original area of animal use either!

One way of understanding Whataboutisms and charges of hypocrisy is through an appeal to consistency. Consistency is a desirable quality for arguments and logic. Calling out hypocrisy could be seen as wanting to apply a standard more consistently. Before veganism was more widely known than it is now, people who would be protesting one form of animal use such as meat eating or fur would get asked 'what about those leather shoes you are wearing?' Quite often they wouldn't be leather but the idea behind this is appealing to more consistency. The difference is it's not coming from a vegan that has put the idea of more consistency into practice but from a critic using it in a fallacious manner.

Whataboutisms are a call for consistency that the people using them lack.

 A better understanding of veganism would once again help prevent many arguments of this sort.

The myth of vegan perfectionism means it is mischaracterised and strawmanned as being a silver bullet for all problems. If it is compared to a perfect solution of removing all animal suffering in the world then of course it is not able to achieve this goal. This is no reason the reject the possibilities of what it can do and the areas it does achieve its aims. Veganism covers the areas of animal use and exploitation so other solutions to problems outside these areas have to be proposed for those areas. To dismiss veganism because it can't solve all problems is as unfair as dismissing any other solution because they can't remove all difficulties or be a perfect solution.

It's sometimes useful to look at an argument we are presented with and think how it would apply in an analogous human rights or environmentalist context. Sometimes when comparing it to whether someone would use those same arguments against an organisation that is rescuing dogs can be very illuminating.

Would people comment on websites about rescuing dogs that it is futile because not all dogs are rescued?

In human rights would people comment that solving one rights violation is useless because other problems will remain?

We live in an imperfect world where animal exploitation is ubiquitous and firmly embedded in cultures and traditions. I have written how the situation we find ourselves in is like Neurath's Boat.

'We are like sailors who on the open sea must reconstruct their ship but are never able to start afresh from the bottom. Where a beam is taken away a new one must at once be put there, and for this the rest of the ship is used as support. In this way, by using the old beams and driftwood the ship

can be shaped entirely anew, but only by gradual reconstruction.'
Neurath, Otto (1973) [1921]. "Anti-Spengler". Empiricism and Sociology. Vienna Circle Collection. (6)

Tu Quoque

This fallacy is also related to Whataboutisms.
'Tu Quoque' is Latin for "you also" or "you're another". I explore one example of this type of argument in Chapter Six on 'Reflexive Arguments' where the response to vegans saying animals are slaughtered is to say vegans are also responsible for animal deaths through modern methods of harvesting crops and protecting crops from animals.
It is a fallacy because pointing out that the person using the original argument is also guilty of something similar does not refute the original point they are making.
'The tu quoque fallacy occurs when one charges another with hypocrisy or inconsistency in order to avoid taking the other's position seriously.' (7) The counter that is aimed at the person making the original claim does not invalidate their claim. This is true whatever the relative severity or seriousness of either the original claim or counter-claim are.

Categorising anti-vegan arguments

With kind permission, I will use **Vegan Sidekick**'s debate guide as a reference to FAQ's. You can see that they are already grouped thematically. The reader can refer to the guide for Vegan Sidekick's answers to these frequently asked questions. I will however offer an analysis of the questions and which fallacies they employ and what category of argument they fall into. As the list is quite comprehensive this should cover most areas. (8)

It doesn't harm animals to kill them
It doesn't harm animals to take their eggs
It doesn't harm animals to take their milk
But cows need to be milked right?
It doesn't harm animals to take their wool
It doesn't harm animals to take their silk
It doesn't harm animals to take their honey

This first category is what I would term 'but what's wrong with ____?' These sort of questions are natural from non-vegans who haven't been familiarised with the vegan position of non-exploitation. The questions may be framed as 'what's the harm?' so answers on that basis try to explain the various ways animal use leads to suffering and harm to animals. We must remember that it is use that is opposed and that the various forms of harm and cruelty to animals are symptoms of the exploitation of animals. We can get too caught up in attempts to create hierarchies of various cruelties to animals when all areas of use can be avoided rather than tackling individual symptoms. Often people will deflect and ask why vegans don't protest some egregious form of animal cruelty that the person opposes. This is an attempt to distance themselves from being involved in animal suffering and harm. It's a form of whataboutism from the Ricky Gervais school of animal advocacy. The bad things are done by other people in other countries and we don't look at what happens every day in our own country. Veganism is of course inclusive of all the areas people already oppose. It would be counterproductive for vegans to concentrate on the areas that most people in the UK aren't involved in and already oppose. It would raise more support as people can virtue signal about things they don't have to make any changes for and don't support anyway. Good for fundraising but not for social change.

Many vegetarians are unaware of the exploitation slaughter involved in dairy and egg production. Vegan Sidekick explains as follows

'In the egg industry, only females are required because males don't lay eggs. As such, in the breeding process, the males and females are divided when they hatch, and the males are killed immediately as they serve no purpose. Subsequently, their sisters go on to be kept in captivity until their egg production is no longer profitable to the farmer, at which point they have their throats slit. This is generally at around one or two years old. The average lifespan of a chicken is eight years.

In the dairy industry, only females are required because males don't produce milk. Like all mammals, cattle produce milk to feed their young once they give birth. It is a misconception that cows just produce milk non-stop, they do so only once impregnated. As such, when a male is born, he will be slaughtered. Either he is culled immediately, or he is sold into the veal industry and then killed after a few weeks of living in confinement, or he is sold into the beef industry and killed as soon as he reaches a profitable size, which will be about one year old. If the calf is female, typically she will be removed from her mother so that the milk can be stolen, and then she is used in the same manner. Once a mother's milk production is less profitable, she has her throat slit. That generally happens after two milking cycles, when she would be around six years old. The average lifespan of a cow is about twenty years.'

The best way to understand what happens to animals in the exploitation industries is through observation and to pay more attention to what farmers and slaughterers do rather than what they say. 'Dominion' is a free to watch documentary and there are sites like 'Standard Legal Practice on Irish Farms' that document the experience of farmed animals.

Our ancestors did it
We've got canine teeth
Lions do it
Circle of life
It's natural
God put animals here for us to kill, bible says so
It's been happening for hundreds of years
We have to eat animal products to survive

These are fallacies of relevance. Rather than going into detail on each question we can simply ask how 'Argument X' is an argument for exploiting and slaughtering animals. The burden of proof is on the person making the claim to demonstrate how their argument is relevant to how animals are used in our time and place. Most of these arguments end up be mere observations, they are descriptive, not prescriptive. They rely mainly on appeals to nature, so observations of how things are in nature to justify how humans should act. If we take the example of someone saying 'humans have canine teeth though' we first need to establish whether this is just a random observation or some sort of argument for slaughtering animals. We can ask how having some teeth means we are obligated to kill and consume animals. This exposes the absurdity of the observation. It is not generally a good use of time to argue about human anatomy at length when simple questions can cut to the core of the issue. Some Socratic questions can help get to the point. 'Why don't slaughterhouse workers use their canine teeth?' 'How does having certain teeth obligate us to use and slaughter animals?'

An **appeal to nature** is a fallacy because being 'natural' is not the relevant factor in deciding whether something is good or bad. This must be decided by other means. Something can be from nature but could be harmful or beneficial. The same is true with **appeal to tradition** (it has been done for a long time) or **appeal to popularity** (everybody is doing it). The problem with these arguments is going from a simple observation to saying 'therefore' we should continue these practices. That is a not demonstrated by a mere description of how things were or are.

Cherry picking. You can of course point out the many herbivorous species that also possess canine teeth that are much more impressive than any human examples, gorillas and hippos come to mind. This cancels out the variable of possessing canine teeth as being relevant or obligatory. This story is similar for other anatomical features. Sometimes people will say we have forward facing eyes which is an anatomical feature of predatory animals with binocular vision. Never mind the fact that our colour vision and forward facing eyes – like those of fruit bats, likely evolved to identify ripe fruit of various colours, and we have the evolved dexterity to pick fruit and nuts. While evolution is one of my favourite subjects it would only be relevant to vegan arguments if it mandated a particular diet. It is sufficient for veganism that we can be vegan. The cherry picking is seen in singling out the behaviour of other animals that people want to justify (meat eating) and ignoring the other behaviours that we do not seek to justify – infanticide, sniffing each other's butts etc. Why is only one behaviour of animals chosen and used as a justification? ''Whenever a debate on veganism arises, there is a very high probability that the discussion will turn to lions.'' – Charles Horn

You could call this **'Horn's Law'** analogous to **Godwin's law** which asserts that "as an online discussion grows longer, the probability of a comparison involving Nazis or Hitler approaches 1.'' Don't worry, Hitler frequently arises in vegan discussions too (see discussion further in chapter.)

Vegans should avoid committing any appeal to nature fallacies also. For our purposes it is sufficient that we can be healthy on a plant-based diet and aren't obligated to consume any animal-based foods.

They're bred to be killed so it's fine
They wouldn't have been born without farmers, we did them a favour

This line of argumentation is known as The Logic of the Larder, a phrase coined by Henry Salt for his essay of the same name. It is a post hoc rationalisation for animal slaughter. It may be one of the most disingenuous arguments in existence. Pretending that breeding and then slaughtering animals at a small fraction of their natural lifespan so you can eat them or consume their eggs and milk is because you are concerned about 'giving them a life' or preserving species. (9)

Breeding animals just to be slaughtered at the earliest possible age is not 'giving them a life'. It's clear that the animal's life and sentience are not the priority. In fact animal sentience is a massive inconvenience to animal farmers. It's odd that they don't admit this and acknowledge that most of their problems are due to dealing with sentient animals rather than non-sentient plants. Compare caring for a dog to caring for a houseplant. The interests and needs of the sentient dog are far greater and the capacity for harm and suffering is present with the dog. To find a real example of 'giving an animal a good life' we must look at animal sanctuaries. Animals here are cared for by humans and allowed to live a life free from exploitation and slaughter. When the claims of 'humane' farmers are compared to real humane treatment of animals at sanctuaries it is clear that the sanctuary is the real model of compassion and a life lived to the fullest possible extent. Not treated as a mere commodity and slaughtered at the most profitable time for the human. A greater model always exposes the limitations or lies of a smaller model. Imagine a sanctuary that gives animals a full life and then decides to kill the rescued animals to make a profit. Or imagine a scenario where you gain a wild animal's trust bit by bit by feeding them and gradually letting them get acclimatised to you. After their initial jumpiness they now trust you. You then decide to kill them one day when they are relaxed enough for you to take them by surprise. Are any of these scenarios 'humane' or fair'?

The 'humane paradox' becomes inescapable. In his excellent video on the subject, David Oates of Veganism Unspun analyses how people argue that animals have a great life – but then take away that 'great life' from the animal. (10) In the scenario where death could arguably be a relief from suffering – the problem remains because it is then the life filled with the cruelties they say they are against. The best way to avoid such false dilemmas presented by people who only give you two options of 'humane' slaughter or worse slaughter and worse conditions is to go for a third option of not breeding and slaughtering animals in the first place.

When did animal agriculture promoters start having to promote 'humane slaughter'? When the public became more concerned about slaughter they then had to launch public relations campaigns and employ a lot of language that sought to reassure consumers it was a good thing. However slaughter itself is never promoted pro-actively as a positive thing. The idea of adding 'humane' to it to make it an oxymoron is to ameliorate the negative aspect of slaughter, but it is still a negative action overall. If this wasn't the case why would it need a modifier to make it sound better? If slaughter is a regrettable necessity that you are trying to make as good as it can be under the circumstances, what happens if you remove the necessity? It just becomes a regrettable action that you don't need to be doing or attempting to make 'better'. As Matthew Scully said "When you start with a necessary evil, and then over time the necessity passes away, what's left?"

Biodiversity

Linked to the concerns over 'species preservation' of the Logic of the Larder is the issue of biodiversity. There are around 40 domesticated species used by humans and of these there are 5 or 6 that represent the vast majority of animals that are exploited and slaughtered. So when people talk about 'species preservation' they are talking about a handful of species whose members vastly outnumber the individuals from many of the species most under threat from human activity.

Science has identified perhaps 1.7 million species out of the possible existence of anything between 3 to 100 million species according to lower and higher estimates. This puts the supposed concern for 'preserving species' where there of millions of individuals in existence into perspective. Usually people may say they are talking about rare breeds of domesticated species. They never suggest sanctuaries or wildlife refuges for these species however, their existence is predicated on killing them, not giving them free lives. If the only reason you are breeding animals is to kill them then you are more interested in their deaths than their lives. Ironically for those with a faux concern for 'species preservation through eating animals' biodiversity of a wider range of species is threatened mostly by meat eating.

''Diets rich in beef and other red meat can be bad for a person's health. And the practice is equally bad for Earth's biodiversity, according to a team of scientists who have fingered human carnivory—and its impact on land use—as the single biggest threat to much of the world's flora and fauna. Already a major cause of extinction, our meat habit will take a growing toll as people clear more land for livestock and crops to feed these animals, a study in the current issue of Science of the Total Environment predicts.'' (11)

''The consumption of animal-sourced food products by humans is one of the most powerful negative forces affecting the conservation of terrestrial ecosystems and biological diversity. Livestock production is the single largest driver of habitat loss, and both livestock and feedstock production are increasing in developing tropical countries where the majority of biological diversity resides.

Biodiversity conservation: The key is reducing meat consumption.'' (12)

''Wild animals suffer not only the collateral damage of meat-related deforestation, drought, pollution and climate change, but also direct targeting by the meat industry. From grazing animals to predators, native species are frequently killed to protect meat-production profits. Grass-eating species such as elk, deer and pronghorn have been killed en masse to reserve more feed for cattle. Important habitat-creating animals such as beavers and prairie dogs have been decimated because they disrupt the homogenous landscapes desired by livestock managers.'' (13)

''Currently, cropping and animal husbandry occupy about 50 per cent of the world's habitable land. The rapid expansion of animal farming has been behind much of this land expansion. Since 1970, the collective weight of wild mammals has declined by 82 per cent, and indicators of vertebrate abundance have shown rapid decline.''

"Instead of wild animals, a small number of farmed animal species (mainly cows and pigs) now dominate global biomass. Together, they account for 60 per cent of all mammal species by mass, compared to 4 per cent for wild mammals and 36 per cent for humans. Farmed chickens now account for 57 per cent of all bird species by mass, whereas wild birds make up 29 per cent of the total. Animal farming now occupies 78 per cent of agricultural land globally" "A global shift to a plant-based diet would substantially reduce the requirement for pasture and cropland (taking into account human nutritional needs and population growth to 2050); such land could thus be spared for nature.'' (14)

What about tribes who have to hunt to survive?
What if you were on a deserted island?
If you get bitten by a snake you'd take antivenom!
But would you use medicine to save your life?

These are arguments from postulated areas of absolute necessity. However, as we saw with the vegan definition, if properly understood with good faith and a principle of charity, it already has accommodation in saying 'as far as is possible and practicable' which is an acknowledgement of the fact we live in a world where we are surrounded by animal use that is ubiquitous. If we apply the test of transferring the argument to a human rights context, would human rights be invalidated because sometimes we have to practice self-defence against humans? The law and human rights make accommodations for self defence. So do our interactions with other animals in situations where we absolutely have no option but to defend ourselves or practice survival.

One of the best answers I saw to the question about Deserted Islands was by Andrew Kirschner and it taught me a lot about how to turn these questions around.

'If you were alone on a deserted island with a pig, would you eat the pig or starve to death? Hmm. If you were not alone, living on a planet with 7 billion people, had access to unlimited fresh fruits, vegetables, nuts, beans, and other healthy foods, and knew animals suffer and die horrible deaths so you could eat them when you don't need to eat them to survive, would you continue to eat them? The difference between our questions is that your scenario will never happen and mine is the choice you face right now. Which do you believe is worth answering?' (15)

The Vegan Society advice on medications is to take them. 'Vegans avoid using animals 'as far as is practicable and possible'. This definition recognises that it is not always possible to make a choice that avoids the use of animals. Sometimes, you may have no alternative to taking prescribed medication. Looking after yourself and other people enables you to be an effective advocate for veganism.'
Many medications are available in vegan form and labelling and awareness is improving all the time. It's something I've raised with my MP and something he acknowledged needs improving.
With greater numbers of vegans the demand for vegan medications will get greater.
 Isn't it a sign of progress to go from using animals to using bacteria to then using flowers to obtain insulin? (16) In terms of animal testing there are promising innovations in 'organs on chips' that can successfully replicate human organs in miniature and provide more accurate models. (17)

Using arguments from extreme situations to justify non-extreme situations is a fallacy.
 It is similar to how Tweets go viral that use a formula of *Extreme Situation That Only Applies In Very Specific Circumstances X Everyone It Doesn't Apply To Liking And Sharing It Using It As A Justification For Animal Slaughter = Viral Tweet Liked By More People Than It Can Possibly Apply To.*

Targeting vegans

Many articles that begin 'Sorry Vegans…' target the 1-2% of the population that are vegan when the implications of the arguments in the article actually should apply to everyone. So why are vegans targeted specifically? Maybe it's an attempt to counter vegan claims as vegans are more vocal about the issues. It could psychological factor of assuaging guilt and complicity about the issues by implying vegans are bad and so can't possibly be right, and so they don't have to be listened to.

Bacon versus lettuce.

Media outlets know that veganism is a hot topic and can generate many more times their usual post engagement and comments. Click bait titles have become common and even journals that are usually impartial become victims of confirmation bias and sensationalism when it comes to veganism.
Dan Nosowitz reported on one such study 'whose press release boldly claimed that lettuce produces more greenhouse gas emissions than bacon' and 'went through a very particular arced news cycle: First the blogs and other publications reported it as written, then a few days later, others (including us) figured out that both the press release and the study itself had serious problems.'

But it takes scientists a bit longer to craft a proper response, so it's only this week that researchers from Johns Hopkins published their letter to the editors in the current issue of Environment Systems and Decisions, the same journal that originally published the contentious study.'

The exultant reporting that 'lettuce is worse for the environment than bacon' is just one example of the eagerness with which anything promoting animal exploitation is promoted to a credulous audience eager to hear good things about animal slaughter and bad things about vegans.

Modern Farmer reports 'The authors of the response seem almost horrified that the study and its press release might imply to casual consumers of science and food news that a vegetarian diet could be more harmful to the environment than a meat-based diet. "Contrary to the media's misinterpretation of the science, the climate impact of pork is over four times higher per serving than vegetables. Dairy's impact is over five times higher, and the impact of meat from ruminant animals (e.g., beef) is over 23 times higher," reads the response's own press release. And the response concludes on a hard note: 'In the USA, there is considerable political opposition to addressing climate change, and strong cultural barriers to reducing meat consumption. Sending a message indicating meat may be a preferable food choice, without adequate supporting evidence, runs counter to climate mitigation efforts and the best interests of future generations.' (18)

This is a familiar pattern to vegans who are generally the only ones willing to counter such claims. There is a scientific paper. It gets reported and spun in some way to target vegans and say something negative about veganism – usually ignoring the other conclusions of the paper. There is some pushback but by then the damage is already done – as Jonathan Swift said 'it often happens, that if a Lie be believ'd only for an Hour, it has done its Work, and there is no farther occasion for it. Falsehood flies, and the Truth comes limping after it; so that when Men come to be undeceiv'd, it is too late; the Jest is over, and the Tale has had its Effect'. Journalists need to do better when it comes to veganism. Unfortunately there are few consequences for the spread of such misinformation. The desired effect of greater engagement on social media posts has been reached. A retraction hardly ever follows and if it does it won't have the same audience. (19)

Vegans are targeted for things like the use of supplements. It can't possibly be just vegans buying all the health supplements in stores, the majority of which are not suitable for vegans in any case.
Vegans are targeted over consumption of soy, avocados, quinoa and other plant foods. The issues from plant agriculture should not be dismissed. But targeting vegans when most soy is used for animal feed is out of proportion to reality. Around SIX PERCENT of all soy grown worldwide is used for direct human consumption. Obviously vegans are not responsible for consuming all of that 6% either as that feeds the entire world including Asia where it is consumed more widely and has been for 3,000 years. The other 94% is split between industrial uses and animal feed, with 70% going to feed animals. The proportions of soy grown in the Amazon for animal feed are even higher. (20)

We therefore have the strange situation of people using other people's situations of dire necessity which might apply at most to 0.5% of the population to justify animal slaughter for the other 99.5%.

And in a sort of inversion of this we have people blaming the 1-2% population of vegans for all the issues and problems that apply to everyone but for which vegans can't possibly be solely responsible for.

The whole world will never be 100% vegan
One person can't make a difference
You can't be 100% vegan in modern society so why bother

These are Nirvana Fallacies and the perfect solution fallacy.
The Nirvana fallacy was given its name by economist Harold Demsetz in 1969 who said:

The view that now pervades much public policy economics implicitly presents the relevant choice as between an ideal norm and an existing "imperfect" institutional arrangement. This nirvana approach differs considerably from a comparative institution approach in which the relevant choice is between alternative real institutional arrangements.

A Nirvana Fallacy occurs when a proposed solution (veganism) is rejected because it is not up to the standard of a proposed solution that is not actually achievable. The Nirvana that is proposed is an ideal norm – in the case of arguments against veganism it means zero harm caused to animals, zero impact on the environment etc. Veganism is rejected because it can't hope to meet these impossible standards. This fallacy ignores the fact that the real world choices do not involve one that can meet the ideal norm.

As Demetz says, our real world choices are between actual existing institutions and systems or at best some arrangement we can come to ourselves but which will still fall short of any ideal norm. The fallacy lies in the rejection of a practical method because it doesn't meet an impossible standard. The Perfect Solution fallacy is closely related and states that the solution should be rejected because some problems still remain even if you adopted that solution. If this fallacy is used then we would never implement any health and safety measures or risk assessments just because we can't guarantee a perfect outcome or solution. This really is letting the perfect be the enemy of the good. It's another example of how anti-vegans want you to just become despondent and think that if you can't avoid *all* harm then you shouldn't avoid the areas of harm that you can.

They want to create confusion and make all choices appear the same. After all, if everything causes harm why not just have a free-for all on causing harm?

Edward Everett Hale writing in 1902 stated,

I am only one,
But still I am one.
I cannot do everything,
But still I can do something;
And because I cannot do everything,
I will not refuse to do the something that I can do.

This is a beautiful quote to remember. Just because we can't avoid every harm caused to other animals just from our existence doesn't mean we shouldn't avoid the areas we can, like meat and dairy and the use of animals for clothes, cosmetics and entertainment. Neither does harm in one area justify harm in another. We are taught early in our lives that 'two wrongs don't make a right'. Anti-vegans however love to play areas of harm off against each other, justifying one harm because others can't be avoided. Apologist vegans do this also.

Questions which can then arise along this line of thought are where to draw the line and just how far can we take the idea of minimising harm? These are very difficult questions. I've seen questions about whether vegans should be morally obligated to calorie restrict. People may also say 'if you were really committed you would live in a hut in the forest'. So now who is making veganism more difficult? We are trying to promote a practical way of minimising animal exploitation and slaughter in the world. Anti-vegans then make excessive demands of vegans and aren't even taking these first practical steps, but talk about going completely off grid, bartering with neighbours and growing all your own food. It's doubtful they actually have any anarcho-primitivist ambitions but if they do, good luck to them. People are welcome to advocate that way of life but not use it as a nirvana fallacy while not practicing it themselves.

People already say veganism is restrictive or difficult but they want to impose even more strictures. I'd say these conversations are for people to have once you are avoiding the most obvious and more easily avoidable areas.

If you aren't even avoiding meat and dairy why would you be interested in ever diminishing returns on avoiding certain calorie sources? Avoid meat and dairy first, then we can talk.

This is touched upon in an excellent Grist article. (21)

''What are the most sustainable vegetables?

By Eve Andrews on Nov 21, 2019

Dear Umbra,

I want to know which grains and vegetables are most sustainably grown. Should I eat more oats? Soup with barley? Squash or sweet potatoes?

— Yearning for Ultimate Minimum

''for all the fretting about "food miles" and eating local, transportation only makes up about 11 percent of a given food's carbon footprint in the United States. (But try to avoid food flown in on a plane, like winter asparagus from South America.) About 80 percent comes from a food source's time in the field, or greenhouse, or feedlot.

But again: In the grand scheme of the carbon or water or land impact of your diet, the subtleties in vegetable and grain farming are — may you and God both forgive me for this one — kind of small potatoes! When it comes to lowering dietary emissions, "the big levers that you can pull aren't sourcing vegetables and grains from a certain farm," says Richard Waite, an associate with the World Resources Institute's food program. "It will be eating more vegetables and grains and moving those toward the center of the plate, and less animal proteins."

The biggest levers you can pull are avoiding meat and dairy.
In answering what the most sustainable vegetables are is worthwhile once you are vegan. As the author of Meat

Logic Charles Horn says, if science argues that people should be cutting way back on animal consumption to only be a tiny fraction of what it currently is, but at the same time it's not an argument that would get people as far as being vegan, he would add "Don't worry, I'll still be here to fight you on that remaining fraction on purely animal rights reasons".

We may not know exactly where to draw the line – in fact it may stretch on much further. But we know for certain which areas are 'above that line' that we definitely can avoid. If you are talking about more difficult areas given the society we live in and the grey areas without avoiding the 'black and white areas' then your words lack the power carried by vegans who are actually practicing avoiding those areas.

If everyone went vegan, livestock would overpopulate
If everyone went vegan, livestock would go extinct
Those animals would just be killed in the wild anyway
You're putting people out of jobs because of the effect on the industry
Vegans have no effect on anything

These are an **appeal to negative consequences** and in the case of 'vegans having no effect' a contrary view that it makes no difference (so choose an option). One appeal is to the supposed loss of jobs from an economy becoming plant based. There are historical precedents for people having to adapt to new technologies and gain different employment. New green technologies have been shown to have great potential for boosting economies and employment. Many people who worked in one old technology can find employment in the new. It's not an argument against the new innovations but rather a case for how more training and help to find employment should be provided, Many farmers have been able to make the switch from animal agriculture to plant agriculture with numerous examples of them going from raising cows to growing oats and from confining chickens in warehouses to growing mushrooms in their place. This needs to be encouraged and the farmers need to be helped to make a transition to more ethical and ecological farming. Subsidies to meat and dairy should be cut and all the externalities of them reflected in a true price of the products. Subsidies should be increased for fruit and vegetables and to help farmers make the shift. No one is arguing for unemployment just better employment. I don't think truckers are going to be bothered about transporting tofu instead of live pigs as long as they still have a job.

One question that is sometimes raised that is a good practical concern is what to do with a lot of agricultural waste that is a by-product of current crop production. A portion of this is used for animal feed and so the question is how to use it for other purposes and not leave crop residue unused as waste. Mushroom cultivation is a good use as it creates another food source. Many crop residues make excellent substrates for growing mushrooms. Other uses are residue being incorporated into building materials and made into pulp and chemicals. When residue is left on the land it is proven to be effective in protecting soils against erosion and improving water retention. When incorporated back into the soil it can greatly enhance soil organic matter. (22) The difference here is that anti-vegans are looking for problems in order to maintain the status quo whereas vegans look for solutions and alternatives to animal use. Many innovations come about this way if only we are willing to think differently and adjust our attitude. Vegan leathers aren't 'just plastics'. Many inventive people have found ways of using crop residue to create vegan leathers from pineapple cellulose (Pinatex), from mushrooms (Muskin), from cacti and from the wine, coffee and various fruit and vegetable industries. When people say vegan leathers are plastic they are lying by omission if they neglect to mention the many truly plant-based alternatives and fail to highlight the environmental damage of leather production.

If everyone went vegan...

People often want to highlight supposed negative consequences of switching to veganism but rarely look for the positives and opportunities that it would represent. Many of these arise simply from no longer propping up a massively inefficient system. Minimising land use also represents a great opportunity for rewilding and offsetting carbon. Following is a list of some of the articles I cite the most to show the opportunity public health savings, the environment, the economy, from a shift to veganism.

"The scientific targets set out by this Commission provide guidance for the necessary shift, recommending increased consumption of plant-based foods – including fruits, vegetables, nuts, seeds and whole grains – while in many settings substantially limiting animal source foods.

This report builds upon a growing body of research pointing to the sweeping benefits of shifting diets. This research has shown that a global shift toward healthier, more sustainable diets will combat climate change and food insecurity, improve human health save nearly 11 million lives globally, make national supply chains more resilient to shocks reduce the financial risks associated with meat production, reduce the risks of future pandemics and could unleash USD 4.5 trillion in new business opportunities each year, at the same time saving USD 5.7 trillion a year in damage to people and the planet" (23)

''Today, and probably into the future, dietary change can deliver environmental benefits on a scale not achievable by producers. Moving from current diets to a diet that excludes animal products has transformative potential, reducing food's land use by 3.1 (2.8 to 3.3) billion ha (a 76% reduction), including a 19% reduction in arable land; food's GHG emissions by 6.6 (5.5 to 7.4) billion metric tons of CO_2eq (a 49% reduction); acidification by 50% (45 to 54%); eutrophication by 49% (37 to 56%); and scarcity-weighted freshwater withdrawals by 19% (−5 to 32%) for a 2010 reference year. The ranges are based on producing new vegetable proteins with impacts between the 10th- and 90th-percentile impacts of existing production. In addition to the reduction in food's annual GHG emissions, the land no longer required for food production could remove ~8.1 billion metric tons of CO_2 from the atmosphere each year over 100 years as natural vegetation re-establishes and soil carbon re-accumulates, based on simulations conducted in the IMAGE integrated assessment model. For the United States, where per capita meat consumption is three times the global average, dietary change has the potential for a far greater effect on food's different emissions, reducing them by 61 to 73%.'' (24)

'Plant protein foods—like lentils, beans, and nuts—can provide vital nutrients using a small fraction of the land required to produce meat and dairy. By shifting to these foods, much of the remaining land could support ecosystems that absorb CO2, according to a new study appearing in the journal Nature Sustainability.' (25)

'In a study published in the Proceedings of the National Academy of Sciences, Marco Springmann and his colleagues at the University of Oxford conservatively estimate that if people continue to follow current trends of meat consumption, rather than shifting to a more balanced or plant-based diet, it could cost the U.S. between $197 billion and $289 billion each year—and the global economy up to $1.6 trillion—by 2050. (The Atlantic) (26)

The natural climate solution with the largest potential to sequester carbon globally is reforestation, with zero new deforestation only achievable though veganism. (27)

'A new study published by researchers at the Institute of Social Ecology has found that it is possible to feed the world without further deforestation. Published in Nature Communications, the study assesses the likelihood of 500 various options for feeding the global population in 2050 in a hypothetical world of zero-deforestation, depending on combination of key factors including agriculture technology, livestock systems, and human diet. Every combination in which the human population follows a plant-based diet would be feasible for a deforestation-free future, the study found. "According to our analysis, human nutritional behavior is the most important component," study author Karlheinz Erb said. "If the world's population followed a vegan diet, all combinations of parameters, even those with lowest yield levels and low cropland expansion, would be feasible.'' (28)

'With a third of all food production lost via leaky supply chains or spoilage, food loss is a key contributor to global food insecurity. Demand for resource-intensive animal-based food further limits food availability. In this paper, we show that plant-based replacements for each of the major animal categories in the United States (beef, pork, dairy, poultry, and eggs) can produce twofold to 20-fold more nutritionally similar food per unit cropland. Replacing all animal-based items with plant-based replacement diets can add enough food to feed 350 million additional people, more than the expected benefits of eliminating all supply chain food loss.' (29)

In 'The carbon opportunity cost of animal-sourced food production on land', study author Matthew Hayek says 'animal feed croplands and pasture compete with native ecosystems and their potential to draw down CO_2'.

'Extensive land uses to meet dietary preferences incur a 'carbon opportunity cost' given the potential for carbon sequestration through ecosystem restoration. Here we map the magnitude of this opportunity, finding that shifts in global food production to plant-based diets by 2050 could lead to sequestration of 332–547 $GtCO_2$, equivalent to 99–163% of the CO_2 emissions budget consistent with a 66% chance of limiting warming to 1.5 °C.' (30)

'The food system is responsible for more than a quarter of all greenhouse gas emissions while unhealthy diets and high body weight are among the greatest contributors to premature mortality. Our study provides a comparative analysis of the health and climate change benefits of global dietary changes for all major world regions. We project that health and climate change benefits will both be greater the lower the fraction of animal-sourced foods in our diets. Three quarters of all benefits occur in developing countries although the per capita impacts of dietary change would be greatest in developed countries. The monetized value of health improvements could be comparable with, and possibly larger than, the environmental benefits of the avoided damages from climate change.

What we eat greatly influences our personal health and the environment we all share. Recent analyses have highlighted the likely dual health and environmental benefits of reducing the fraction of animal-sourced foods in our diets. Here, we couple for the first time, to our knowledge, a region-specific global health model based on dietary and weight-related risk factors with emissions accounting and economic valuation modules to quantify the linked health and environmental consequences of dietary changes. We find that the impacts of dietary changes toward less meat and more plant-based diets vary greatly among regions. The largest absolute environmental and health benefits result from diet shifts in developing countries whereas Western high-income and middle-income countries gain most in per capita terms. Transitioning toward more plant-based diets that are in line with standard dietary guidelines could reduce global mortality by 6–10% and food-related greenhouse gas emissions by 29–70% compared with a reference scenario in 2050.' (31)

'A new study published by researchers at the Institute of Social Ecology has found that it is possible to feed the world without further deforestation. Published in Nature Communications, the study assesses the likelihood of 500 various options for feeding the global population in 2050 in a hypothetical world of zero-deforestation, depending on combination of key factors including agriculture technology, livestock systems, and human diet. Every combination in which the human population follows a plant-based diet would be feasible for a deforestation-free future, the study found. "According to our analysis, human nutritional behavior is the most important component," study author Karlheinz Erb said. "If the world's population followed a vegan diet, all combinations of parameters, even those with lowest yield levels and low cropland expansion, would be feasible." In contrast, only 15 percent of the 500 options that include a global meat-heavy diet would work toward the goal of preservation of forests. The findings follow a similar highly publicized study that found more than eight million lives and $1 trillion in healthcare costs could be saved by the year 2050 if the world adopted a plant-based diet.' (32)

Regenerative agriculture

As already stated the greatest opportunity for carbon sequestration on land is through re-forestry.

'Multiple production and demand side measures are needed to improve food system sustainability. This study quantified the theoretical minimum agricultural land requirements to supply Western Europe with food in 2050 from its own land base, together with GHG emissions arising. Assuming that crop yield gaps in agriculture are closed, livestock production efficiencies increased and waste at all stages reduced, a range of food consumption scenarios were modelled each based on different 'protein futures'. The scenarios were as follows: intensive and efficient livestock production using today's species mix; intensive efficient poultry–dairy production; intensive efficient aquaculture–dairy; artificial meat and dairy; livestock on 'ecological leftovers' (livestock reared only on land unsuited to cropping, agricultural residues and food waste, with consumption capped at that level of availability); and a 'plant-based eating' scenario. For each scenario, 'projected diet' and 'healthy diet' variants were modelled. Finally, we quantified the theoretical maximum carbon sequestration potential from afforestation of spared agricultural land. Results indicate that land use could be cut by 14–86 % and GHG emissions reduced by up to approximately 90 %. The yearly carbon storage potential arising from spared agricultural land ranged from 90 to 700 Mt CO_2 in 2050. The artificial meat and plant-based scenarios achieved the greatest land use and GHG reductions and the greatest carbon sequestration potential. The 'ecological leftover' scenario required the least cropland as compared with the other meat-containing scenarios, but all available pasture was used, and GHG emissions were higher if meat consumption was not capped at healthy levels.' (33)

Carbon sequestration

Climate Myth...

Holistic Management can reverse Climate Change

"Holistic management as a planned grazing strategy is able to reverse desertification and sequester atmospheric carbon dioxide into soil, reducing atmospheric carbon dioxide levels to pre-industrial levels in a period of forty years." (Allan Savory, 2014)'

Climate Fact - 'Multiple scientific studies from climate scientists and agricultural specialists show little or no significant gain in carbon sequestration on soils managed holistically to those with other grazing techniques. Even under the most favourable conditions, Holistic Management (HM) alone can only slow climate change by a small percentage, over a limited period, and certainly cannot reverse climate change.'

Skeptical Science (34)

'Multiple production and demand side measures are needed to improve food system sustainability. This study quantified the theoretical minimum agricultural land requirements to supply Western Europe with food in 2050 from its own land base, together with GHG emissions arising. Assuming that crop yield gaps in agriculture are closed, livestock production efficiencies increased and waste at all stages reduced, a range of food consumption scenarios were modelled each based on different 'protein futures'. The scenarios were as follows: intensive and efficient livestock production using today's species mix; intensive efficient poultry–dairy production; intensive efficient aquaculture–dairy; artificial meat and dairy; livestock on 'ecological leftovers' (livestock reared only on land unsuited to cropping, agricultural residues and food waste, with consumption capped at that level of availability); and a 'plant-based eating' scenario. For each scenario, 'projected diet' and 'healthy diet' variants were modelled. Finally, we quantified the theoretical maximum carbon sequestration potential from afforestation of spared agricultural land. Results indicate that land use could be cut by 14–86 % and GHG emissions reduced by up to approximately 90 %. The yearly carbon storage potential arising from spared agricultural land ranged from 90 to 700 Mt CO2 in 2050. The artificial meat and plant-based scenarios achieved the greatest land use and GHG reductions and the greatest carbon sequestration potential. The 'ecological leftover' scenario required the least cropland as compared with the other meat-containing scenarios, but all available pasture was used, and GHG emissions were higher if meat consumption was not capped at healthy levels.' (35)

Arguing at the margins

Another argument you may hear on land use is that animal agriculture uses land which is unsuitable for crops which is a strange way of spinning the fact that animal agriculture maximises land use by using land that could otherwise be performing more valuable ecological services such as being native forest. The assumption is that all land needs to be used for some human purpose and providing a service to humans. It ignores the fact that a vegan model would minimise land use and so not every piece of land would need to be used. Instead it could be re-wilded and returned to nature. As we have seen this provides greater opportunities for carbon sequestration than the dubious claims made by holistic grazing advocates.

As Lorelei Plotczyk of Truth Or Drought writes 'The land used to grow crops for people to consume directly (vegan food) supplies more calories and protein for the global population than the almost 4-times larger area used for animal agriculture (Our World in Data). Yet there remains an allegiance to the idea of using marginal lands to graze ruminants for consumption. This doesn't hold up, because the paltry yields don't justify the negative impacts. A vegan shift would free up such land for conservation and other purposes, including growing hardy human-edible plants.

To graze farmed ruminants, staggering amounts of land is used for incredibly little return. For example, about 60% of the world's agricultural land is used for "beef," which only accounts for less than 5% of protein and 2% of calories worldwide (Union of Concerned Scientists). A portion of that land is considered marginal.

"While 'grassfed' animals may not be dependent on arable-based feeds, the supposition that they are using spare land that could not be used for something else is mistaken... land that is used to graze animals could potentially be used for something else – for food, for nature conservation, for forests, or for bioenergy." (Grazed And Confused Report).
' (36)

Marginal land arguments only make sense when you see that it is farmers, with a vested interest in continuing to use that land that way and also maintain shooting estates for hunters, who are making the case for continuing their livelihoods in the only way they have known on that particular land.

Contradictions

As people haven't thought through the consequences and the facts about what currently causes the problems cited, we are often faced with contradictions. You will notice how fearing an overpopulation of domesticated animals is then followed by the concern with those animals going extinct. This pairing is often called Schrödinger's Cattle, I don't know who coined the term but thank you. Once people learn the answer to why animals that are being bred in massive numbers wouldn't overpopulate or be running free if they simply were not bred anymore their faux concern shifts to non-existent animals. A question to ask people so they arrive at the answer themselves is where do all the animals come from at present? If vegans don't support breeding animals how would this problem then arise?

Relevant to this are also the contradictions in people who say the world won't go vegan overnight but then fearing the drastic consequences of such an overnight shift. Their own criticism, if they stick to it, holds the answer. A shift to veganism on a population level may take generations. In this time industries cease breeding and slaughtering animals and shift to plant based alternatives. The fears of job losses and any drastic consequences are therefore answered.

People do however argue that veganism would mean a mass 'cull' of animals and I have seen this referred to as a 'genocide' of animals. Clearly they think there would be one final slaughter of all animals and they object to this strongly. It is strange then that they don't object to this 'final' slaughter being repeated in perpetuity. Why should the finality of a mass slaughter be so abhorrent but a continual cycle of it receive such enthusiastic support? It's hard to imagine that this is actually a genuine concern of those supporting a continuous cycle of slaughter. Veganism is merely breaking this cycle.

'These animals have better lives than those born in the wild.'

Saying the animals would be killed in the wild also touches on the current situation for animals and the answer. People will say the animals would suffer and be killed in worse ways by predators in the wild. This assumes that the animals bred to be slaughtered would ever find themselves in the wild. This is an impossibility except for a lucky few animals that escape from slaughterhouses. Their stories usually inspire great sympathy and goodwill. However animals bred for slaughter will never be free in the wild to face any such natural hardships or predation. It is a false dilemma where the options are a death in a slaughterhouse or a death in the wild and the latter option is not even a possibility! Animals bred for slaughter are trapped in what is essentially a 'canned hunt'. Just as lions are bred and confined so they can more easily be killed and a kill is guaranteed, so too are all domesticated species. The history of domestication shows how early humans came across this solution from corralling animals they used to hunt and gradually interfering more in their lives to control reproduction and movement. Eventually it developed along different pathways one of which is the prey pathway which is the canned hunting element– breeding and confining animals to ensure a guaranteed kill – eliminating the need for hunting wild animals. Talk of canned hunting being better than a life in the wild is therefore a fallacy.

This argument states that as animals in the wild can suffer from predation, disease and injury and that animals that are bred on farms are looked after by humans and protected from predators and given help or avoid most natural calamities. In a way it is similar to The Logic of the Larder argument. However there really isn't a causal relationship as with that argument. First of all 'natural predators' are simply replaced by human predators. They may want to think of themselves as 'caregivers' in this case but ultimately the animals are bred to be killed in what amounts to a canned hunting operation.

In the case of arguing for animals - that are artificially inseminated, born and confined for their lifespan of anything from one day to a few weeks or months or at most around a quarter of their natural lifespan and then violently slaughtered by human predators- being spared the travails of a life in the wild, we have to ask how exactly they are being saved from this? There is no causal link where if they are not bred and slaughtered they will suffer the fates described in nature. So while it's true they will avoid being killed by predators it is also true that this is simply not something that could happen to them anyway as their whole existence is within the confined limits of exploitation by humans. It would be like saying breeding and slaughtering humans 'saves' them from being killed by old age and disease. Well, yes, I suppose, but it's hard to see how they are linked by cause and effect – the 'saving' is not saving if it's not something that could happen to you. These animals will never be in the wild. The argument can only mean that they think slaughter by humans is

preferable to a worse death in nature. This is an absurd justification for slaughter and could be used to justify any hypothetically worse thing than the slaughter you are defending. It is a false dilemma to say the only two options are a death in the wild or a death at the hands of humans. It is an example of the attempt at 'advantageous comparison' described in chapter three – making something bad appear better through comparison to something worse.
A question to ask those using this argument may simply be 'how does breeding, confining and slaughtering animals save them from a death in the wild?'

Animals are killed in crop harvesting so vegans kill more animals
In Australia, grass-fed beef is more ethical than eating wheat
Plants have feelings

These arguments and those about any issues involving use of resources are the ones that backfire due to ecological efficiency and trophic levels. Any problems you can point to in plant agriculture are magnified by not minimising land use.
Chapter Six on reflexive arguments covers the issue of crop deaths of animal from harvesting.
Attempting to turn vegan arguments back on themselves is doomed to failure and reminds me of people trying to prove perpetual motion machines can work through circumventing the Second Law of Thermodynamics. These arguments lead to trying the reflexive arguments or seeking loopholes and extreme exceptions that exist outside of the usual laws of energy transfer between trophic levels. There is no evidence that plants are sentient and even if they were

it would still be better to consume fewer by eating lower on the food chain. (37)

Don't force your opinions on others
Stop judging me
A vegan was rude to me once

These arguments are more thought terminating cliches. We all make value judgements about issues. If people don't want to have their motives or morality examined they attempt to make it out of bounds. 'Non-judgement' is such a tactic. There are ways of talking that are more 'judgemental' than others in tone. However, there is no real neutrality on the issue and judgements are being made by you whether you are conscious of them or not. The irony is that they are often not short of judgement about vegans during the course of a conversation. Anticipated moral reproach can make a person feel 'judged' just through the presence of a vegan.
Don't people arguing a position think their position is 'better' and aren't they making implied 'judgements' about morality and the quality of arguments? Just because you don't like vegan advocacy doesn't mean you can pretend you are somehow free from an ideology yourself or are a neutral observer of arguments without thinking you know best too. Otherwise why are you offering your opinion?

Concentrating on individual vegans rather than on other animals and how they are exploited is the diversionary tactic that people like to employ to avoid addressing what happens to animals.

"Veganism is not about vegans. Vegans are people with all sorts of good and bad points. But that says nothing about veganism. Vegans are often the messengers of veganism, but don't confuse the two. Veganism is the understanding that animals value their own lives and bodies, that animals have an interest in continuing their existence and avoiding suffering and that animals have the right to be treated with respect and justice and not to be treated as property. The logic of veganism stands independent of any individual vegan person."
– Greg McFarlane

Rudeness and hostility should be avoided and we can see where arguments lie on Graham's hierarchy. However using such arguments to justify animal slaughter is tone policing and shooting the messenger. Plenty of vegans have been rude and obnoxious to me but I am not going to take that out on the animals. (38)

**There are wars going on / people starving in the world
Yeah but sweat shops and slave labour**

Other issues

These issues may be related to alternatives. These may be tu-quoque attacks but I think we have to guard against being defensive. Avoiding meat and dairy are the 'big levers' we have already pulled and the most effective practical first steps in minimising impact on animals and the environment. Other issues such as transport, electricity use and problems within plant-based agriculture or plastic use and the like are real issues and should be acknowledged. We can ask how consuming animal products or supporting animal exploitation helps any of these issues. How does eating bacon help farm labourers? These other issues are of course not unique to vegans and not necessarily avoided by non-vegans. If non-vegans are somehow avoiding these areas that are much more difficult to avoid than simply going vegan they are welcome to advocate for them and lead the way in showing how to do so. How many of the practical methods will necessitate animal exploitation and slaughter?

If the non-vegan can therefore avoid these areas already there is no reason why they can't also avoid them when they go vegan. If it is shown that it's possible while working and living in our society and also meets the criteria of not exploiting animals which does not help those issues then the example set by non-vegans in avoiding these areas can also be followed by vegans. This is assuming these are issues the person arguing actually cares about.

Balance Fallacy

We see examples of this fallacy with anti-evolutionists and climate change deniers who say to 'teach the controversy' where none actually exists. Media outlets will typically invite people on programmes to offer 'balance' on matters of science that are settled. This is a false idea of balance. It's often seen with vegan debates where the idea of not exploiting and slaughtering animals has to be 'balanced' by those who profit from commodifying animals or deny the climate impacts of animal agriculture. A recent article from The National Trust for Ireland is excellent in highlighting this false notion of balance. (39)

The appeal to moderation is another sort of balance fallacy where the assumption is that the true or correct position must lie between two other positions at different ends of a spectrum. (40)

For those who think of veganism as 'extreme' it is natural to fall into this way of thinking. Vegetarians often style themselves as being 'in the middle' between vegans and meat eaters as if they are in a more objective position and able to therefore moderate a debate between the two. Eating cheese doesn't however automatically confer powers of greater impartiality in the debate. Anyone thinking they are in a more neutral or objective position because they support animal use is kidding themselves. The appeal to popularity confers an aura of objectivity because things that agree with what most of society supports are seen as more objective or neutral. Status Quo bias also plays a part in this. Vegetarians tend to side with meat eaters more than vegans in discussions – agreeing with vegans would imply the need to be vegan. However they can agree with areas of some meat-eaters arguments that suit them like any things that position veganism as extreme or undesirable.

We don't think the reasonable position lies somewhere in the middle when it comes to slavery, child abuse or other human rights issues.

Tom Regan said it best when he said

'The position that we hold — the abolitionists position — is often said to be "extreme," and those of us who hold it are said to be "extremists." The unspoken suggestions are that extreme positions cannot be right, and that extremists must be wrong.

But I am an extremist when it comes to rape — I am against it all the time. I am an extremist when it comes to child abuse — I am against it all the time. I am an extremist when it comes to sexual discrimination, racial discrimination — I am against it all the time. I am an extremist when it comes to abuse of the elderly — I am against it all the time.'

Decision Point Fallacy -

Many fallacies are used with the intention of you not being able to make a decision – continuum fallacy/where to draw the line/ false equivalence fallacy/ balance fallacy/Nirvana fallacy/appeal to futility are all of this nature in blurring lines and distracting us from the areas where we are more certain and have more control.

They are all linked by this obfuscation of facts and attempts to sow confusion, as if there isn't a scientific consensus around ecological efficiency, climate change, animal sentience, the health of plant based diets etc. Rather than promote something pro-active themselves the opponents of veganism that bring up other problems are actually happier if you were to go back to the thought terminating clichés of chapter one and take morality out of the equation.
This is not possible when there are victims and we must never forget the animals.

The 'No Ethical Consumption...' Argument

This argument says that 'there is no ethical consumption under capitalism' and therefore veganism is not a worthwhile choice. The argument is really a Fallacy of the Gray. (41)
It is saying there is no *absolute* ethical consumption under the system but ignoring the *relative* differences. In saying things aren't black and white they replace a two colour scheme with a one colour scheme – everything is unethical so no different choices are relevant or differentiated. From saying things aren't dualistic they go to saying everything is one undifferentiated unit. It is nonsense to say we can't distinguish areas that are lighter than darker areas even if we can't say exactly where one shade becomes another. A relative difference in consumer choices does exist. It also frames veganism as a consumer activity only and narrows it down in this way to argue more effectively against a strawman version.

Once again, it serves only to defend the status quo unethical consumption whilst people imagine they are 'dismantling capitalism' whilst not even being able to change their breakfast.

Some anti-vegan arguments prove more popular than others at different times. It can depend on the audience as to how they are interpreting veganism and through which moral framework. If they are hostile to veganism they will use their framework as the set of tools to argue against veganism (and for animal use and slaughter even where this is avoidable). They lump veganism in with whatever things they are used to arguing against and think veganism has those problems intrinsically too. Where there are practical issues in shifting society and individuals to veganism this should be acknowledged. But it should also be acknowledged that there are individuals and organisations aware of practical and social justice issues and working to overcome these barriers. There are also Indigenous, poor and disabled vegans who should not be erased by ignoring their voices. These groups of people and their real situations should not be appropriated by those who are not in the same circumstances to argue for animal use that can be avoided.

Notes to Chapter Four

(1) Baloney Detection Kit - http://www.inf.fu-berlin.de/lehre/pmo/eng/Sagan-Baloney.pdf
(2) "Write to Be Read: Reading, Reflection, and Writing, 2nd ed." Cambridge University Press, 2005
(3) https://tvtropes.org/pmwiki/pmwiki.php/Main/AppealToWorseProblems
(4) https://www.theguardian.com/books/2015/sep/25/industrial-farming-one-worst-crimes-history-ethical-question

Air quality–related health damages of food
https://www.pnas.org/content/118/20/e2013637118

https://www.independent.co.uk/climate-change/air-pollution-health-animal-farming-b1844921.html (5)
https://rationalwiki.org/wiki/Not_as_bad_as
(6)
https://www.academia.edu/11084757/Neuraths_Boat_and_Veganism
(7) https://www.thoughtco.com/tu-quoque-logical-fallacy-1692568
(8) Vegan Sidekick FAQs
http://www.godfist.com/vegansidekick/guide.php
(9) https://www.henrysalt.co.uk/library/essay/logic-of-the-larder/
(10) Veganism Unspun - Humane Paradox
https://www.youtube.com/watch?v=4XFVS2S1fN0

See also Humane Hoax - https://humanehoax.org

Your Vegan Fallacy Is - https://yourveganfallacyis.com/en/humane-meat/resources

Doris Lin - https://www.treehugger.com/arguments-for-and-against-humane-meat-127672

(11) https://www.sciencemag.org/news/2015/08/meat-eaters-may-speed-worldwide-species-extinction-study-warns
Biodiversity conservation: The key is reducing meat consumption
https://www.sciencedirect.com/science/article/abs/pii/S0048969715303697

(12) How Eating Meat Hurts Wildlife and the Planet
https://www.takeextinctionoffyourplate.com/meat_and_wildlife.html
(13) Humans' meat consumption pushing Earth's biggest fauna toward extinction
https://www.sciencedaily.com/releases/2019/02/190206101055.htm
(14) - Food System Impacts on Biodiversity Loss
https://www.chathamhouse.org/2021/02/food-system-impacts-biodiversity-loss
Plant-based diets crucial to saving global wildlife, says report
https://www.theguardian.com/environment/2021/feb/03/plant-based-diets-crucial-to-saving-global-wildlife-says-report
Human carnivory as a major driver of vertebrate extinction
https://www.sciencedirect.com/science/article/pii/S2530064420300614
http://trophiccascades.forestry.oregonstate.edu/human-carnivory-project
(15) https://kirschnerskorner.com/2013/03/15/if-you-were-alone-on-a-deserted-island-with-a-pig-would-you-eat-the-pig/
(16) https://www.popsci.com/science/article/2010-02/first-pigs-then-bacteria-now-insulin-flowers/
(17) https://sciencenordic.com/biology-denmark-medicine/human-organs-on-chips-may-one-day-replace-animal-testing/1443448
(18) https://modernfarmer.com/2016/03/bacon-lettuce-greenhouse-emissions/
(19) Truth or Drought is a great resource for analysing the media responses to certain scientific papers and how they spin them to target vegans. https://www.truthordrought.com/lettuce-vs-bacon-myths
(20) https://www.onegreenplanet.org/environment/why-tofu-consumption-is-not-responsible-for-soy-related-deforestation/
(21) https://grist.org/ask-umbra/what-are-the-most-sustainable-vegetables/

See also 'Organic meats found to have approximately the same greenhouse impact as regular meats' https://phys.org/news/2020-12-meats-approximately-greenhouse-impact-regular.html
(22) https://www.iadb.org/en/news/15-million-new-jobs-2030-transition-net-zero-emission-economy-idb-and-ilo-say

Further reading - Crop Residues: Agriculture's Largest Harvest: Crop residues incorporate more than half of the world's agricultural phytomass
Vaclav Smil
https://academic.oup.com/bioscience/article/49/4/299/228907

(23) https://www.bmj.com/content/370/bmj.m2322
(24) Reducing food's environmental impacts through producers and consumers

J. Poore & T. Nemecek

https://science.sciencemag.org/content/360/6392/987

(25) - Changing what we eat could offset years of climate-warming emissions, new analysis finds https://phys.org/news/2020-09-offset-years-climate-warming-emissions-analysis.html
(26) https://www.theatlantic.com/business/archive/2016/03/the-economic-case-for-worldwide-vegetarianism/475524/4146

see also https://interactive.carbonbrief.org/what-is-the-climate-impact-of-eating-meat-and-dairy/

(27) Natural climate solutions -
https://www.pnas.org/content/114/44/11645

https://www.carbonbrief.org/analysis-how-natural-climate-solutions-can-reduce-the-need-for-beccs

see also https://interactive.carbonbrief.org/what-is-the-climate-impact-of-eating-meat-and-dairy/

(28) Feeding the world without further deforestation is possible
https://www.sciencedaily.com/releases/2016/04/160419120147.htm

See also https://ourworldindata.org/world-lost-one-third-forests

(29) https://www.pnas.org/content/115/15/3804 The opportunity cost of animal based diets exceeds all food losses
Alon Shepon, Gidon Eshel, Elad Noor, and Ron Milo

https://www.nature.com/articles/s41893-020-00603-4#:~:text=In%20high-income%20countries%2C%20in,their%20domestic%20fossil%20fuel%20emissions

(30) https://www.nature.com/articles/s41893-020-00603-4?proof=t
(31). Analysis and valuation of the health and climate change cobenefits of dietary change
http://m.pnas.org/content/113/15/4146.full

http://www.pnas.org/content/113/15/4146.abstract

More analysis -

Cornell - http://allianceforscience.cornell.edu/vegan-diet-mitigates-global-climate-change

Oxford - http://www.oxfordmartin.ox.ac.uk/news/201603_Plant_based_diets

https://timesofindia.indiatimes.com/life-cycle-analyses-shows-a-plant-based-diet-is-most-nutritious-with-least-environmental-impacts/articleshow/80176375.cms

(32)
https://www.sciencedaily.com/releases/2016/04/160419120147.htm
See also Options for keeping the food system within environmental limits by Springmann et al -
https://www.theguardian.com/environment/2018/oct/10/huge-reduction-in-meat-eating-essential-to-avoid-climate-breakdown#:~:text=Huge%20reductions%20in%20meat-eating,times%20more%20beans%20and%20pulses.

(33) Nature - https://www.nature.com/articles/ncomms11382

See also - Chatham House - https://www.chathamhouse.org/publication/livestock-climate-change-forgotten-sector-global-public-opinion-meat-and-dairy

(34) Food and Climate Research Network of Oxford University -

http://www.fcrn.org.uk/research-library/protein-futures-western-europe-potential-land-use-and-climate-impacts-2050

Grazed and Confused report - https://www.oxfordmartin.ox.ac.uk/news/2017-news-grazed-and-confused/

Grazed and Confused video - https://www.youtube.com/watch?v=nub7pToY3jU

Holistic Management: Misinformation on the Science of Grazed Ecosystems - https://www.hindawi.com/journals/ijbd/2014/163431/

https://skepticalscience.com/holistic-management-rebuttal.html

https://www.sierraclub.org/sierra/2017-2-march-april/feature/allan-savory-says-more-cows-land-will-reverse-climate-change

https://skepticalscience.com/holistic_management_climate_change-advanced.htm

(35) Food and Climate Research Network of Oxford University -

http://www.fcrn.org.uk/research-library/protein-futures-western-europe-potential-land-use-and-climate-impacts-2050

(36) Marginal Land Myths – Truth Or Drought
https://www.truthordrought.com/marginal-lands-myths#:~:text=Marginal%20lands%20myths%20—%20Truth%20or%20Drought&text=Source%3A,use%20gives%20us%20in%20return

UK could slow climate clock by converting animal farmland to forest and still grow enough protein. New research from Harvard University demonstrates that the UK would be able to sustain itself and help meet the Paris Agreement by returning a portion of land used for animal agriculture back to forest. Converting land currently used for grazing and growing animal feed crops back to forest could soak up 12 years' carbon emissions

https://www.thelondoneconomic.com/news/environment/128436/11/04/

Assessing the efficiency of changes in land use for mitigating climate change

Timothy D. Searchinger, Stefan Wirsenius, Tim Beringer & Patrice Dumas

https://www.nature.com/articles/s41586-018-0757-z

Can Britain Feed Itself?

https://www.thelandmagazine.org.uk/articles/can-britain-feed-itself#:~:text=In%201975%2C%20the%20Scottish%20ecologist,template%20for%20making%20similar%20calculations.

Impact of a vegan agricultural system on land use

https://www.veganaustralia.org.au/impact_of_a_vegan_agricultural_system_on_land_use

(37) Plants Neither Possess nor Require Consciousness
https://www.cell.com/trends/plant-science/fulltext/S1360-1385(19)30126-8

(38) http://thethinkingvegan.com/people-are-not-vegan-because-of-you/
(39) Beware of 'balance' claims in agri debate - https://www.antaisce.org/balance-claims-agri-debate
(40) https://en.wikipedia.org/wiki/Argument_to_moderation
(41) https://www.lesswrong.com/posts/dLJv2CoRCgeC2mPgj/the-fallacy-of-gray

Chapter Five

Variables

Relevant and irrelevant variables.

If there is one key concept that I always keep in mind it is identifying and analysing variables and how relevant or irrelevant they are to an argument. You or your opponent's argument may be right or wrong but not for the reasons given or the argument that is presented. The easiest way to assess this is whether the variable used in the argument is relevant and has any bearing on whether what you are trying to prove or conclude with your argument is valid and true. This forms the basis of fallacies of relevance.

The 'variables' are the elements of your argument. In scientific experiment the variables of things which affect the outcome of the experiment. So amount of time, temperature, pressure, materials etc are variables. The type of fuel used to heat a beaker of water would be a variable if the experiment was to see which fuel heated the water to boiling point in the shortest time. By changing only the variable of fuel used and not the amount of water the irrelevant variables in the experiment would be any extraneous factors that do not have any bearing on the outcome of the experiment. For a fair result we must maintain the consistency of the other variables so we can isolate the variable we want to test. So fuel is changed in each experiment but not the material of the beaker or the purity of the water. By isolating variables we see which ones are relevant.
Analogously we can isolate variables in arguments and see if they are relevant to our conclusion.

Talking past each other.

We must bear in mind that vegans and non-vegans are starting from different standpoints and perspectives. Vegans will most often be thinking about animals as victims of animal exploitation and slaughter. So when an anti-vegan is offering up an argument it is seen as a justification for animal use and slaughter when alternatives and avoidance of it is possible. Saying you like the taste of bacon therefore immediately seems extremely callous when it is viewed from the perspective of the exploitation confinement and slaughter this will cause to an animal, in this case gas chamber suffocation for pigs, regarded as the most 'humane' method. Most anti-vegans say 'mmm, bacon' not 'mmm, animal slaughter'. Non-vegans tend to start from their own perspective of consumer choice. Whereas vegans are looking at the whole life-cycle of an 'animal product', non-vegans will concentrate on the end-product only, not wanting to consider the full life-cycle if possible. The source of their consternation with vegans is therefore wondering why they are being questioned about just another ingredient or a menu item. Starting from these different perspectives, vegans and non-vegans are often talking past each other. One side is looking at any excuse or argument as a direct justification for animal slaughter. Non-vegans are thinking they don't need to justify a menu choice or a shopping trip. They don't consider shopping or meal times a moral issue. Once again it is framed as personal choice and morality kept off the table if possible. Non-vegans often think they are arguing against a personal dietary preference rather than arguing against animal rights and think they are arguing for consumer choice rather than supporting animal use and slaughter.

Framing

How we express our initial arguments can determine responses to a large degree because they are framing the discussion. If we were to discuss veganism as a diet only we should not be surprised if the responses are replies along the lines of talking points of personal dietary preference, fad diets and the like. We should look for the strongest way to frame our initial argument which will prevent misunderstandings, diversions and irrelevancies. A framework of justice is the best I have come across. It is harder to argue against the fact that animals are unfairly exploited and are victims of an injustice.

So with the idea of where vegans start from – a framework of justice and seeing any arguments or excuses presented against veganism as justifications for animal use and slaughter against we can see just how irrelevant many of the arguments against veganism are.

To take a few of the most common that are presented we see how absurd they appear from the standpoint of a justice movement. If someone was arguing for human rights and was detailing how sweatshops exploit workers it would be extremely callous for someone to comment that they didn't care, they just like the end product too much. This is exactly what we see with arguments from taste however when it comes to animal rights.

In terms of the variables of veganism it is whether animals are used, exploited and slaughtered which is what we find relevant. Animals are worthy of moral consideration because they are sentient. Other variables are not morally relevant because sentience is the determining factor on whether causing pain would be wrong. Sentience means animals can be victims, there is a being who can experience positive and negative states and so inflicting harm upon them has consequences for them.

Whether an animal is 'treated nicely' for a few days but then slaughtered at the youngest possible age is irrelevant compared to the fact they are exploited and slaughtered. Other variables may compound the whole situation but it is the exploitation and slaughter of sentient beings which is wrong at a fundamental level. This is drawing the line further than most humans who don't consider sentience the relevant factor or the act of exploitation and slaughter the relevant factors. For them it depends on the species or the intelligence of the individual and some forms of treatment are unacceptable but others aren't and exploitation and slaughter is acceptable depending on species.

For the example of cosmetics we may have two products A and B where A is produced by not testing on animals and B is produced by testing on animals. For our example we assume all other variables are equal. So the price, availability and quality of the cosmetic are all the same and the variable that is particular to product B is animal testing – therefore causing animal suffering being a particular demand of B that isn't present in product A.

When it comes to food there are more variables that are relevant because the production involves factors such as crop deaths, transport, greenhouse gas emissions, price and availability that are currently present in plant food production. It is not as easy to isolate one variable such as 'testing on animals' and have all other things being equal in the real world. For food production there could be an ideal where the only variable is animal exploitation and If we say our aim is to improve things then we should all be seeking to have the variables equalise or improve on the 'vegan side' so that price, availability, transport emissions etc are better than on the animal-based food side. This is already true when it comes to all variables, so whilst not perfect, plant-based choices are superior but there is always room for improvement.

The reason to equalise the variables is to make the choice as clear as in the case of the cosmetics products A and B. But even where variables are not exactly equal the choice of being vegan is clearly better.
In terms of entertainment we can also draw an easier line and say not using animals is more easily avoidable as most people now consider other forms of entertainment more wholesome and find using animals for entertainment or fighting immoral. The more relevant variables an argument has the better. If the argument is about practical aspects then variables about price availability and access to plant-based food are the relevant factors and arguments with those as the focus will be valid. We should seek to improve price, availability and access in order to equalise the variables and make the only relevant variable that is different the fact of animal use and slaughter. As in the case of cosmetics the choice is between only one variable. Who would choose to use and slaughter an animal when this is the only variable that is different between two options?

Food Shapes

The question of which variables are in play is a good method for testing each argument we encounter. The vast majority of anti-vegan arguments have been shown to be irrelevant from a standpoint of justice for animals. Canine teeth and what lions do are irrelevant to our choice as humans. Believe it or not, one of the most popular arguments at the time of writing (Zoonotic Pandemic Summer 2020) is 'why do vegans want their food to taste and look like meat?' with the implied or sometimes stated assumption 'if they don't like meat?'

Of course this is the wrong question because it doesn't take into account the actual relevant variable or criteria of why vegans avoid animal products in the first place- to avoid animal use. With that understanding in place the issue of taste and texture etc is not important as long as the variable of concern to vegans is considered. Put another way it isn't taste and texture that are objected to but the exploitation and slaughter of animals.

To turn the question round, why do animal eaters specifically demand the inclusion of animal exploitation and slaughter in their food if they could avoid it? Variables come into play when looking at the common arguments against veganism like the confusion expressed over why vegans want to have products that are the same texture, name or flavour as their animal based counterparts. Analysing it from the point of view of the variables involved we see that for the vegan the most important variable is animal use and slaughter. The anti-vegan misses this point either on purpose or through not being able to see that this is the most vital variable. Whether the shape or flavour of some food is similar to another is not an important consideration and from a moral point of view is irrelevant. If two products have variables such as taste, texture, shape all being equal and one is vegan and the other is the product of breeding, confining, transporting and slaughtering animals then why would anyone want to specify the inclusion of animal use and absolutely insist upon this? I don't think people are actually as confused on this issue as they make out. What is hard to understand about wanting to avoid animal use and slaughter but have a familiar taste and texture of a food type to take the place of the food shape that use to occupy that space on your plate? It is also helpful for those

transitioning and makes it easy to substitute a plant based alternative into already familiar recipes or veganising other recipes. Of course the contrast that is brought into focus by comparing these variables is disliked by those who like animal products. They therefore take the focus away from the variables that involve animals and their individuality and lives and to the other end of the process where they are unrecognizable due to having been slaughtered and rendered into food shapes. It's strange that this is the criticism of plant foods when the same amount of processing applies to those animal foods that vegans are accused of mimicking. A burger or sausage made from animals bears as little resemblance to the animals it came from as a burger or sausage made from plants resemble the original plant it came from. Why the double standard? Are falafels an acceptable shape for food according to anti-vegans or not?
The objection from animal product sellers comes down to competition from plant based alternatives. Companies have never expressed concern about how a sausage doesn't look like a pig before. Hot dogs and burgers or patties are just convenient shapes for food.

Why is the variable of including an animal's life and their food having been sentient so important to them? If it isn't, great, they should eat food that was never sentient.
By looking at which variables are actually relevant most anti-vegan arguments are rendered completely insensible. Why don't slaughterhouse workers use their canine teeth? It's because having those teeth is irrelevant to their work? Now you are starting to get it.

If we don't identify which variables matter and which are actually morally relevant then we can't talk meaningfully about the morality of actions.

It's important that we know what our criteria for moral status and relevance are.

It's rather like conspiracy theorists who believe a lot of conspiracies. Not all of them can be true because some will cancel others out or make others impossible. For any model of the universe like science or religions this is equally true as there will be components to the models that are mutually exclusive and only one can be the correct model. For science it is about continually refining that model. With conspiracies however, what are the variables and criteria people are using if they say one is true but another isn't? Evidence would be the best criteria but this would bring us into the realm of investigative journalism and science in any case. So we would have to suspend judgement until we had enough evidence. This isn't the case with most conspiracies that are just wild speculation. So without the correct variables it is rather like a free for all of conspiracies. If people are saying plants and rocks are sentient then it's a sort of greedy reductionism of morality where you can harm a rock and it's the same as harming a dog. With no criteria to differentiate these actions it is a free-for-all.

This is type of going nuclear too. The moral equivalence that is created is also designed to make all decisions the same and stop any action being decisively taken.

Going Nuclear can also involve being nihilistic or invoking solipsism and extreme epistemological skepticism. It takes down almost the whole of what can meaningfully be said about anything with you but is deemed a price worth paying not to have to deal with veganism.

People raising other issues don't actually care want you to care about them. If you were to say you don't care then that would create the equivalence they seek where we can't make moral judgements, morality is taken out of the equation and we are back to the thought terminating clichés and going in circles trying to pin people down for some criteria of moral concern for other animals.

Leftist Speciesists

Different types of arguments come from different demographics and political persuasions. Whilst the section on psychology highlighted how bogus ideas of masculinity, dominance and hierarchy as well as adherence to tradition and religion are hallmarks of the political right, the left argues against veganism for some different reasons. Although the left will say they are against oppression and hierarchy they make an exception for the billions of land animals and trillions of marine animals that are slaughtered each year. Human supremacy comes in many forms and may be subtler than the gaudy displays of hyper masculinity and patriotism from the right but it is there nonetheless.
Perhaps realizing the fallacious nature of the Frequently Asked Questions, many leftists have retreated or been forced to argue in other areas. They attempt to use identity politics and ideas of privilege and colonialism to argue against the practice and advocacy of veganism.

Veganism is racist, colonialist, and imperialist!

Anti-vegan Leftists will say veganism is about everything *except* ending animal exploitation and slaughter.

Any instances of racism and classism must be taken seriously. There is however nothing inherently racist or classist about veganism.
Vegans come from all races and to characterise veganism as a 'White' thing erases the work of BIPOC vegans and those that are working to make veganism more accessible

in their communities through education and practical help. Many organisations are aware of these types of issues surrounding food deserts and accessibility and seek to address those issues and increase awareness. Why do these critics of veganism never share their stories or their work? Food Empowerment Project and Chilis on Wheels are just two examples of organisations working to educate the public and feed the homeless. The Plant the Land Team Gaza is a vegan food justice/community projects team in Gaza, Palestine who provide vegan food distribution, medication, warm winter clothing/blankets, & engage in community projects such as building village water wells, planting public food forests and gardens, etc. There are many more but you probably haven't heard of them because they don't have the support of people who would rather make their ignorance more widely known than share anything positive.

Veganism has been shown to be cheaper which is an obvious reason plant based foods are favoured for relief efforts worldwide. The lower risks of food poisoning and greater shelf life of these foods is also a benefit. (1) (2)

There is no doubt more education and accessibility is needed but is that something you are using as an argument against veganism or something you are working on improving?

Whatever criticisms are levelled at veganism you can multiply by at least ten due to the factors of trophic level consumption and ecological efficiency if you support animal agriculture.

Slaughterhouse workers are mysteriously left out of viral Twitter posts that target unethical farming practices as is the environmental racism of where pig farms are located. Leaving out a group of marginalized and oppressed beings – the other animals that are exploited and slaughtered by humans - is not progressive. Total liberation without the inclusion of veganism is incomplete.

Imagine looking at the world and thinking vegans are the problem?

It can be useful on occasion to ask people if they are anti-speciesist and anti-animal-exploitation if they seem unable to get past the word 'veganism'. Many Leftist critics of veganism will say they are and they are going to write about it in the future!

To continually eliminate the irrelevant variables and arguments I think we have to keep asking 'is this why you aren't vegan?' when presented with an argument. Another way of framing it is 'Is this (your argument) the reason you support animal exploitation and slaughter?' Or 'how does eating meat and dairy help with the problem you've identified?'
If it renders any of their arguments ridiculous when it's stated like that, it's because they are.
Jeremy Bentham identified the relevant variable for moral consideration in a famous passage from his 1789 Introduction to the Principles of Morals and Legislation. It was a time of revolution and the recognition of human rights and freedoms. Bentham begins by discussing how it has been recognized that the colour of one's skin is not a morally relevant variable when it comes to a right to be free from torture and enslavement. He recognizes that other animals 'sensitive beings', we might say 'sentient beings' these days -

'It may come one day to be recognized, that the number of legs, the villosity of the skin, or the termination of the os sacrum, are reasons equally insufficient for abandoning a sensitive being to the same fate. What else is it that should trace the insuperable line? Is it the faculty of

reason, or perhaps, the faculty for discourse?...the question is not, Can they reason? nor, Can they talk? but, Can they suffer? Why should the law refuse its protection to any sensitive being?'

Fallacies and variables

Many fallacies arise from the use of irrelevant variables in arguments – those that don't determine the actual truth-value of the argument unless it is somehow relevant include who the messenger is, the source (**Genetic Fallacy**), age, appearance, physical strength and many features such as these. The truth is determined in other ways than these unless the question of what is to be proven is about those features.

Relevance is also a main feature of fallacies. Quite often a statement is a fallacy because it is irrelevant to the truth-value of what the statement is hoping to prove. Something may be true or false but it is a fallacious statement if the statement has variables that do not support that conclusion. The truth-value will just have to be proven in other ways. Fallacies can often be paired.

The **appeal to middle ground** says that a position between two other positions is valid by virtue of being in such a middle point. This is not necessarily true as many counter examples from ethical positions that should be absolute can demonstrate.

The **appeal to popularity** says that a position is true by virtue of being held by a majority or a large amount of people. Again this is not necessarily true. Whole populations and cultures have been mistaken in their beliefs. Indeed, if there can only be one true model of reality or people claim only one religion is true this implies the believers in other models and faiths are sorely mistaken. The opposite fallacy would be an appeal to novelty – an idea being true because it is new or is not held by a majority. This is also a **Galileo Gambit** named after people's appeal to the idea that if they are ridiculed or go against the norm it gives their argument validity by this mere fact. As Carl Sagan said "The fact that some geniuses were laughed at does not imply that all who are laughed at are geniuses. They laughed at Columbus, they laughed at Fulton, they laughed at the Wright brothers. But they also laughed at Bozo the Clown."

— Carl Sagan, Broca's Brain: Reflections on the Romance of Science

Sentience

Sentience is the capacity to have conscious experiences. It means a being can be harmed and experience mental states that may be positive or negative.

'**Sentience** is the capacity to feel, perceive, or experience subjectively. Eighteenth-century philosophers used the concept to distinguish the ability to think (reason) from the ability to feel (**sentience**).'

Sentience is not to be confused with 'sapience'. Sapience, literally meaning 'wisdom' as in 'homo Sapiens' (Latin for wise man) is used to denote a level of knowledge and usually self-awareness. Science Fiction has contributed to the confusion on this issue by using 'sentience' where 'sapience' should be used and vice versa. When talking of alien species the writers will say that there are 'no sentient lifeforms on a planet' when in fact there are animal lifeforms that we would regard as sentient. So when people say 'animals are sentient', those confusing it with 'sapience' think it is a mistake as they think other animals don't qualify for sapience. Those that argue for sapience as the morally relevant criteria set the bar too high for moral consideration. In doing so they eliminate concern for sentient beings that should qualify.

If sentience *is* accepted as the morally relevant criteria it can still lead to arguments being used to undermine its relevance to animals. We have seen how 'sapience' attempts to set the bar too high but the bar can be set too low for sentience when it is taken to mean 'living beings'. We can have a reverence for all life but this is a sort of **greedy reductionism** to miss the point of veganism which is avoiding the exploitation of sentient animals by humans. Often people will argue that plants are sentient and can even argue that crystals and rocks have some level of awareness. (3)

This expands consciousness to the realm of inanimate objects where there is no scientific proof or indeed any known physical, chemical or biological structures such as a nervous system which conscious entities have and facilitate conscious awareness. Panpsychism is the doctrine or belief that everything material, however small, has an element of individual consciousness. This is what people are subscribing to when they argue for sentience being present elsewhere than in animals. It's often argued in some religions that there are some elements of consciousness that may be present but not fully activated in plants and materials. However they still make the case that consciousness is developed in animals and that there is a demarcation between plants and animals, with the latter having more fully developed consciousness.

It can lead to a **sorities paradox** as seen in pretending not to know where to draw the line on which species are sentient, as if we can't easily avoid exploiting the species we know with much higher degrees of confidence are sentient. It can lead to solipsistic nihilism where the person can 'go nuclear' and ask 'how do we know any other being is sentient?'

Descartes did not eliminate dog suffering through his declarations that they were automatons any more than modern animal harmers eliminate pig suffering by declaring the animals they exploit to be mere 'production units' or 'livestock. Suffering doesn't magically disappear due to human designations and categorisations.

We see this Greedy Reductionism in Jay Bost's article which won an ethics essay prize. He skips the morally relevant area of concern which is animal use and suffering and reduces everything to transfer of solar energy. This has no explanatory power at the level of concern that is meant to be being addressed. You could say battles between humans are 'energy transfer' but at the cost of explaining the suffering of humans that are being wounded and killed. Bost's style of reductionism could explain away all manner of human experiences and mistreatment. So why is it different when it comes to other animals? All of a sudden his style is awarded prizes. Surely this is only possible when there is a credulous audience wanting desperately to cling to any ideology and explanation that attempts to justify animal slaughter, no matter how fallacious. (4)

Why is sentience the morally relevant criteria?

'The reason that consciousness or sentience is crucial for morality is that experiences, which only conscious beings can have, can be positive or negative for individuals who possess them. They can affect the being for good or ill. A similar way of defining sentience, therefore, is the capacity to be harmed or benefited.' (Animal Ethics)

Sentience is the relevant criteria because it matters morally if a being can be harmed and caused pain. If we examine the reason why it is wrong to torture a dog it is not any of the many characteristics of a dog we can list such as the species they belong to or that they have a certain type of body shape. If it is refined down to the most fundamental level of why it is wrong it is because dogs are sentient – torturing them causes them pain. If we take any sentient species and ask why it would be wrong to inflict pain on them it's because pain can be inflicted upon them. It may sound like a tautology but it can't be for any other reason. It's only self-serving speciesism that has made species membership the criteria used by the majority of humans when assigning relative moral consideration to different individuals. If an animal can be a victim then they qualify for moral consideration. If an individual can be harmed then this matters to their wellbeing. Through 'species overlap' we can draw a type of Venn diagram where the relevant reason it matters to individuals that they can be harmed is because they are sentient. The other characteristics and variables do not fall within the area of why it is ultimately relevant to the individual. If sentient A.I. develops it will matter that they have experiences and wellbeing. If we meet alien species who are sentient it will matter to them that they have experiences and wellbeing.

Additional types of harm such as specific psychological distresses may compound the harms but if they were used as a criteria on their own they would eliminate a whole are of harm and those that can be harmed. Sentience is therefore not an arbitrary criteria unlike others but the very basis of why harm should be avoided and wellbeing promoted. It is why our actions matter towards other conscious beings. Our actions towards non-conscious objects may matter in other ways but even if they are traced back it is because someone will be harmed at the source. A rock can be damaged but not harmed because it has no subjective experience or characteristic to experience harm.

Finding the common ground of sentience gives a firmer footing to a criteria for moral consideration. Animal welfare laws acknowledge animal sentience because it is a recognition that it matters how animals are treated and that they have the capacity to suffer – it is this capacity to suffer that is the reason for any such laws. It is only the imposition of arbitrary gerrymandering lines around certain species that cut them off from equal consideration in comparison to wildlife or dogs and cats. In fact laws such as Customary Farming Exemptions are a tacit acknowledgement of sentience as the morally relevant criteria. They recognise that an extraordinary exception must be made in order to exploit these animals. Otherwise it would be classed as cruelty under law. This doesn't change the experience for the victim, just the ability of the exploiters to use these particular species. Domestication has not removed the relevant characteristics from the species that are exploited by humans.

If sentience is not acknowledged in farmed animals whose 'welfare' is being taken care of?
If you can identify the reason why it would be wrong to harm one animal then you can identify that criterion in other animals.
Unfairness comes from denying this commonality of overlap of relevant characteristics. Those who want to exploit and slaughter look for irrelevant differences between other animals. Those who seek justice and fairness look for morally relevant similarities.

When looking at anti-vegan arguments we have to examine what the variables are. The use of **whataboutisms** brings up other variables and so they have to be weighed. For example, in response to a case for veganism people may bring up slave labour and deforestation. We have looked at the relative impacts of plant-based versus animal based diets and the disparity is great across all these variables due to ecological efficiency. Where the variable is something that would be present in veganism and non-vegan practices then we need practical suggestions to minimize or eliminate any harmful variables. In comparing products we look at the difference in variables in every area and for the whole lifecycle of the product – GHG emissions, land use, water use, pollution, food miles. We see which variables have the most impact and which are equal amongst our choices. Animal exploitation and slaughter are variables that are always present with animal products however. With veganism as the topic, animal exploitation and slaughter will always be a variable that is present and one the animal exploiters do not deal with eliminating or seriously minimizing.

If you say the relevant criteria for moral consideration are being alive or being of a certain species it ignores the individual experience of sentient beings. Ecosystems can be damaged but they do not experience suffering or loss.
Opposition to animal rights concentrates on variables that try to erase the morally relevant criteria that supporters of animal rights use. If we look at the main arguments used against animal rights they attempt to make rights only apply due to conditions that most sentient beings cannot hope to reach. They call for a criteria of species membership, understanding social contracts, social bonds, moral agency and the common sense difference of killing humans vs animals to be the morally relevant factors. (5)
These do not make animal sentience and interests disappear, they just formulate a way to discount them.

People will often bring up areas that are problematic in vegan advocacy or individuals who are vegan and try to use these as arguments against veganism. An analysis on

the basis of variables shows that these are not variables that are inherent to veganism itself.
If you are identifying any problematic variables with vegans or veganism but know it is still possible to be vegan and avoid those problem areas, but you aren't vegan, then you are merely weaponising those issues against other animals to perpetuate speciesism and animal exploitation.
If 'ethical omnivores' were serious about being consistent they would be arguing just as vigourously against those who indiscriminately consume any and all types of animal products as they do against vegans,
they would be providing practical suggestions for improving plant agriculture and advocating for
the minimisation of animal use and slaughter.
This is not what we see however.
Given the fact that it is not practically possible for everyone in a population to follow the high standard the ethical omnivores set due to lack of scalability and the fact that any ramping up or intensification of production defeats their purpose and re-invents intensive agriculture they should actually be supporting vegans as the rest of the population would have to be vegan. Think of it this way, unless the whole population is vegan there is going to be only a certain percentage able to afford or have access to the ethical omnivore standard. Therefore even if their model is one of suffering reduction across the board and elimination of 'factory farming' then the model the rest of the population would be required to follow to allow their overall utilitarian calculation is a vegan one. If 99% of products currently come from factory farms and replacing that demand is impossible – this is why farming intensified in the first place, then the scaled back model can only be followed by either a small percentage or overall production is capped unless it meets their standards. We see very little campaigning for this and animal agriculture supporters are loathe to even answer questions about whether meat and

dairy production and consumption should be reduced. The reality is that the 'humane' labels are there to make humans feel better about their choices and serve as 'halo' products that greenwash and humanewash the rest of the animal agriculture industry. They support the rest of animal agriculture and don't speak out against it or encourage society to avoid it. If they did they know it is a foot in the door for veganism and they are unwilling to concede anything or reduce in any way. Why would they? It is a business at the end of the day.

Once the problem variables are accounted for do they support a 'non-problematic' version of veganism? Are there non-ableist and inclusive versions of veganism possible? Ones that don't use body-shaming, ageism and sexism? If these are not inherent to veganism then once these variables are cancelled out what is the argument then?

It would be interesting to do a frequency analysis of anti-vegan arguments to see which are used most often. As an individual you could just spend time observing conversations on social media and make a note of each argument used and then tally them up if any are repeated.

How does supporting animal breeding, confinement and killing help Indigenous people? We see that these of arguments from Indigenous people's land rights is another area that people themselves are not in unless they are indigenous and those are their personal circumstances.

The Amazon is being cleared for cattle ranching by gangsters who regularly execute environmentalists and burn vast swathes of the forests. Settler colonialism was built on ranching and removing indigenous people to create canned hunting (ranching) operations. Barbed wire changed The West for good and ended the free movement of land animals. Any animal that dares compete with human fishing or cattle ranching is trapped, poisoned or shot. Where is the concern from the people appropriating the position of Indigenous people for the Amazon tribes who are forcefully removed from their land?

How do Indigenous people feel about being used in such a way to justify animal agriculture and the exploitation and slaughter of species that are bred, confined and killed? The question of Indigenous practices is a separate one to the consumption habits of those not in that situation. Yet posts on Twitter go viral and are liked and shared by numbers of people who can't possibly be in those circumstances unless census figures for the Arctic Circle are wildly inaccurate. There is the question of erasing the existence of Indigenous vegans also of which there are many who recognise that once they are in different circumstances the way they choose to live is to be vegan. Climate change which is exacerbated by animal agriculture also adds the final insult in that it endangers the very people living and working in these areas. Climate change disproportionately affects people in developing countries and regions like the Arctic where there are more Indigenous people in those positions being argued about.

I advocate veganism to people who are able to use the same privilege of choice that I have. People love to say 'if it doesn't apply then it's not personally directed at you' but then get hung up on generalised vegan advocacy. How does a general vegan advocacy message hurt anyone?

Religion and other ideologies are used as Escape Hatches to get out of debates and discussions. Imagine if someone said they have to slaughter animals because they are a certain star sign. Invoking unfalsifiable and unverifiable ideologies is no different. Sometimes after a subject has been debated for a while people may use an escape hatch of saying they don't care about the subject. Our society is so far removed from being ethical to animals that the whole point is that you can have the most absurd and illogical argument in order to justify animal slaughter and society will support you, friends and family will support you, every form of media will be on your side and ridiculing vegans if possible. People can confidently say they don't need to justify animal use because they know society will support them. Whether they can actually defend their position is another matter but it is analogous to if someone had protested Gladiatorial games in Rome. The intellectual debate can always be sidestepped through sheer force of consensus and not having to think about it because it is accepted by a majority. Only a society so far removed from fairness can view veganism as extreme and think using and slaughtering animals when it is entirely unnecessary is some sort of 'middle-ground' or 'neutral' position. Wouldn't just leaving animals alone be the neutral position? Then positively helping them represents the only way humans should interfere. The no ethical consumption under capitalism operates as an escape hatch now. Originally it was meant as a way to offer support for people who are forced to make difficult choices despite their best efforts to avoid supporting unethical practices. For example, despite being vegan, our taxes go towards subsidies for animal agriculture. The same is true for our taxes going towards wars and other things we may object to. The idea is meant to be that despite our best personal efforts some things are unfortunately and regrettably unavoidable at present until there is system change. The key part is 'despite our best efforts' not ' we can't make *any* ethical choices may as well support the very worst even though they could be avoided'. In this way the 'No Ethical Consumption' argument has been utilised to excuse any and all consumption through a fallacy of the gray and Nirvana fallacy – may as well eat at McDonalds and pay for Seaworld tickets because of this convenient escape hatch from personal responsibility.

Returning to variables we see that an analysis on that basis shows that even if capitalism was 'dismantled' the variable of animal exploitation and slaughter being an avoidable wrong still remains. It wouldn't suddenly be justified to exploit animals under a communist system.

Here is a summary of some of the ways of analysing the variables in arguments.

Equalising variables – we look at each variable for two models and see if they can be brought into consilience. If there are any outstanding variables then we know we have identified a factor that can't be further equalised.

Isolating variables – looking at one variable at a time we can see how important it is to the overall argument. Would removing it make a difference? Is it possible to remove it and how does this affect the model or the argument?

Cancelling out variables – if someone was saying the best way to advocate s to be friendly, approachable and pragmatic but they are implying these variables belong to advocating fr something other than veganism we can apply 'cancelling out variables'. If it's possible to advocate for veganism whilst being friendly, approachable and pragmatic then we have cancelled those variables out, like we do when cancelling out terms on two sides of an equation. The variable that's left over must be the thing they actually have a problem with.

If the only time problems in plant agriculture are raised is to argue against veganism then this is suspicious. Where there are practical issues in shifting society and individuals to veganism this should be acknowledged. There are plenty of excellent organisations and individuals already working to overcome these barriers. Are they being supported and highlighted or does that not fit the narrative?

General principles

Recognising the type of discussion – the level on Graham's Hierarchy is a good guide
Recognising some features of discussions and how there are 'rules' to productive exchanges
Analysing arguments – being able to identify fallacious arguments and explain why –
Being able to construct logical arguments without using faulty reasoning
And using the principle of identifying variables
through equalising, isolating and cancelling them out to arrive at core issues and morally relevant criteria.

Recognising patterns in arguments – ecological efficiency and trophic levels being a major reason so many anti vegan arguments backfire
Recognising where there is agreement on premises and how this determines the positions adopted -
Reflexive arguments are those that accept more and more premises in common with your position but attempt to turn it back on itself. Seeking acknowledgement that this means agreement up to a certain point at least and calling people's bluff on being consistent with that
Recognising attempts at 'short circuit' arguments' loopholes 'exceptions' etc which also accept the arguments on how systems and ecological efficiency works but seek to circumvent the normal processes in that system
Being able to keep the focus on the core principles and general points and not allowing yourself to be too

distracted by minutiae which may just be a debate tactic to avoid addressing the more general argument. For example, we can discuss which vegetables have the lowest GHG impact, but it should be recognised that this offers ever diminishing returns compared to the best step of removing animal based foods (because even the highest impact plant based foods are lower in impact than the lowest impact animal based foods.)

Recommended reading

Veganism as an aspiration
https://www.wellbeingintlstudiesrepository.org/diecfaori/2/

https://www.wellbeingintlstudiesrepository.org/cgi/viewcontent.cgi?article=1001&context=diecfaori

https://medium.com/@Veganarchy/the-radical-lefts-top-10-objections-to-veganism-and-why-they-suck-5f27d19e801d

https://medium.com/@veganarchistmemes/dear-leftist-critics-of-veganism-veganism-is-not-ableist-or-classist-95d280e0a747

Recommended Resources -

Vegan Media Studies – Christopher Sebastian
Food Empowerment Project
Seed the Commons
A Well Fed World
Chilis on Wheels

Notes to Chapter Five

(1) https://thebeet.com/study-shows-going-meatless-saves-an-average-of-23-per-week-on-groceries/
(2) https://money.usnews.com/money/personal-finance/articles/2016-12-30/how-to-save-money-by-going-vegetarian
(3) Sci-fi may be to blame again here if you've ever seen William Shatner opining about Captain Kirk free-climbing Yosemite's El Capitan. https://www.youtube.com/watch?v=Kestt5BI3eg
See also L. Ron Hubbard and
https://en.wikipedia.org/wiki/Plant_perception_(paranormal)
(4) https://www.nytimes.com/2012/05/06/magazine/the-ethicist-contest-winner-give-thanks-for-meat.html
(5) Animal Rights: A Very Short Introduction pages -23-33

Chapter Six

Reflexive Arguments

In this chapter we will look at what I call 'reflexive arguments' against veganism. They are reflexive because it is as if they agree with the argument up to a point and then turn those very premises back upon themselves to reach a different conclusion. Often that conclusion may seem appealingly counter-intuitive to people who want to argue against veganism.

The Steven Davis Proposal

Part One: Background

In 2003 Steven Davis, professor of animal science at Oregon State University, published a paper in the Journal of Agricultural and Environmental Ethics arguing that it's possible that a plant-based diet could result in more animal deaths due to modern crop harvesting than eating cows who grazed on pasture would.
 The argument isn't as simple as saying vegans are responsible for animal deaths too and so it is better to consume animals. The caveats to Davis' argument are quite specific and must be understood. Davis takes on the assumptions that it is wrong to kill animals and that they are rights-bearers and that it is best to minimise harm and slaughter of animals where possible. Anyone using the argument also has to adopt these premises if they claim to care about the implications.
Davis writes in his abstract

'Based on his theory of animal rights, Tom Regan concludes that humans are morally obligated to consume a vegan diet. When it was pointed out to him that even a vegan diet results in the loss of many animals of the field, he said that while that may be true, we are still obligated to consume a vegan diet because in total it would cause the least harm to animals (Least Harm Principle, or LHP) as compared to current agriculture. But is that conclusion valid? Is it possible that some other agricultural production alternatives may result in least harm to animals? An examination of this question shows that the LHP may actually be better served using food production systems that include both plant-based agriculture and a forage-ruminant-based agriculture as compared to a strict plant-based (vegan) system. Perhaps we are morally obligated to consume a diet containing both plants and ruminant (particularly cattle) animal products.' (1)

There is a trend now of arguments from anti-vegans that tell vegans what they may be obligated to do. Vegans should consume large herbivores or at the other end of the scale they are obligated to consume insects as this would result in less environmental impact. These are reflexive arguments because they attempt to turn the vegan arguments back on themselves in some aspect where it is proposed that the reflected area is what vegans should consume or be doing. It's usually framed in such a way that it's 'if vegans really cared' they would consume insects. However they always ignore the fact that if people were going to the trouble of creating animal based 'solutions' they could also be creating plant based solutions like algae or growing fungi which can be grown in warehouses where otherwise millions of insects would be being farmed. (2) When the person making these arguments has no intention of eschewing all animal products save the ones they insist vegans should be consuming it is hard not to conclude that they are merely playing Devil's Advocate and seeking to trap the vegan in a 'gotcha' where they should consume some animals. Another point is that it shouldn't be 'if vegans really cared' but 'everyone' if we are talking about actual global solutions that will take effect.

Davis uses just two studies to arrive at an estimate for the number of animals that die in plant agriculture harvesting. ''Davis draws his estimates from a study done on field mice in England, and from a study done on sugarcane fields in Hawaii. In the English study, 33 field mice were fitted with radio collars and tracked before and after harvest. The researchers found that only 3 percent of them were actually killed by the combine harvester (amounting to one mouse). An additional 52 percent of them (17 mice) were killed following harvest by predators such as owls and weasels, possibly due to their loss of the crop cover. It is unknown how many of these mice would have been eaten by owls or weasels anyway.'' (3)

Out of 33 mice that were tracked, one was killed by a harvester directly. The other 32 were killed by natural predation or escaping. It's reasonable to think that highly mobile and alert animals such as mice would be able to flee from harvest machinery. It's true that some animals such as fawns do not but in Germany there were initiatives to start spotting the animals lying down in fields. (4) The different behaviours of animals to escape predators suggests ways in which we might help them avoid harvests and help them have warning and escape from fields. As long as the dominant narrative is using these arguments against vegans rather than seeking to minimise harm then solutions are unlikely to be found or demanded. (5)

From these two studies 'Davis estimates that 15 wild animals per hectare per year are killed as a result of harvesting annual crops, and guesses that maybe half that, or 7.5 animals per hectare per year, are killed on grazed land with managed perennial forage.' (Animal Visuals)

Davis continues 'But what of the ruminant animals that would need to die to feed people in the pasture-forage model? According to USDA numbers quoted by Francione (2000), of the 8.4 billion farm animals killed each year for food in the US, approximately 8 billion of those are poultry and only 37 million are ruminants (cows, calves) the remainder includes pigs and other species. Even if the numbers of cows and calves killed for food each year was doubled to 74 million to replace the 8 billion poultry, the total number of animals that would need to be killed under this alternative method would still be only 1.424 billion, still clearly less than in the vegan model.

Davis slyly puts in the current figures for 37 million ruminants slaughtered each year into his calculation for 'pasture fed animals' in his proposed model. This is NOT how the current system produces 37 million slaughtered animals. So doubling that number is not doubling the current system – According to the North American Meat Institute approximately 5% of cows that are slaughtered in the USA are fed on pasture for their whole lives. This 5% model is the one Davis is proposing become 100% in order for his model to work. So this is a bait and switch.

Since Davis made his proposal there have been a number of thorough refutations, especially those by Gaverick Matheny and Andy Lamey. (6) (7)

Animal Visuals summarises as follows "Gaverick Matheny identified a crucial error in Davis's calculation: it assumed that equal amounts of land will produce equal amounts of food from crops or from animals on pasture. In fact, an amount of land will produce much more food when used to grow crops for direct human consumption than when used to raise cattle, provided it is suitable for growing crops. Once Matheny corrected the calculation, Davis's argument made the case for, rather than against, a vegan diet, given an objective to cause the least amount of animal death. Davis's argument was also criticized by Andy Lamey, who pointed out that the case that Davis makes for the numbers of animals being killed by harvesting activity is weak, as his numbers included animals who were killed by predators, and that the argument overlooks ways that humans can be harmed or killed by beef production but not vegetable production." Davis deserves credit for identifying the problem which is harvesting itself. It's not a problem inherent in plant agriculture, but is due to modern methods. It is something that can hopefully be minimised and eliminated. Animal slaughter is an inherent part of animal agriculture which is essentially a canned hunting model of breeding and slaughtering animals for a guaranteed kill. Only by eliminating animal sentience could the inherent problems be removed. That animal sentience isn't more widely acknowledged as a massive inconvenience for animal exploiters is a mystery. Most of their woes are due to the fact they are having to deal with animals with their own interests and consciousness. But if they acknowledge this they are faced with another set of problems in slaughtering animals with interests and acknowledging the sentience which has been denied so long. Matheny's rebuttal notes

that Davis's argument fails on three counts: first, Davis makes a mathematical error in using total rather than per capita estimates of animals killed; second, he focuses on the number of animals killed in production and ignores the welfare of these animals; and third, he does not count the number of animals who may be prevented from existing.
 Davis calculated the total number of animals killed from current systems.

''Davis mistakenly assumes the two systems – crops only and crops with ruminant-pasture – using the same total amount of land, would feed identical numbers of people (i.e., the US population). In fact, crop and ruminant systems produce different amounts of food per hectare – the two systems would feed different numbers of people. To properly compare the harm caused by the two systems, we ought to calculate how many animals are killed in feeding equal populations – or the number of animals killed per consumer.''

Davis is using the same total amount of land for his 50% plant based 50% pasture based system and this makes the calculations off by an order of magnitude of the difference in ecological efficiency between plant-based and animal-based agriculture.

The most economical use of land that feeds the maximum amount of people from that land would be the model that minimises harvest deaths. Merely calculating the current number of deaths and then saying a vegan model would use that same amount of land and therefore be causing deaths due to land use ignores the fact that a vegan model would use the least amount of cropland, when the land that is suitable for edible crops is used to grow food for direct human consumption. Not all crops are equal in the amount of land they use to provide a certain amount of calories

When Matheny recalculates using Davis' formula he finds that "to obtain the 20 kilograms of protein per year recommended for adults, a vegan would kill 0.3 wild animals annually, a lacto-vegetarian would kill 0.39 wild animals, while a Davis-style omnivore would kill 1.5 wild animals. Thus, correcting for Davis's math, we see that a vegan population would kill the fewest number of wild animals, followed closely by a lacto-vegetarian population."

As the author of 'Unpopular Vegan Essays Contrasting Harms: Vegan Agriculture versus Animal Agriculture' writes -
''Matheny's calculation is referring ONLY to wild animals (i.e. only those animals inadvertently killed in crop land or pasture). A "lacto-vegetarian" population would, as a practical and economic matter, kill significantly more total animals, including ruminants, than a vegan population since 1) vegans don't kill ruminants, and 2) ruminants, like humans, do not produce milk without being pregnant, which would lead to a massive glut of unusable male calves and "spent" dairy cows which have outlasted their lacto-productivity, a productivity ending several years before their life expectancy terminates…when we account for the "disposal" of the excess ruminants, we see that a "lacto-vegetarian" population moves away from the vegan population and closer to the Davis-style omnivore population in terms of all animals killed.'' (8)
As Matheny notes to properly compare the harm caused by the two systems, we ought to calculate how many animals are killed in feeding equal populations – or the number of animals killed per consumer – this makes more sense than just comparing two arbitrary amounts of land and

calculating number of deaths from those amounts of land. We should look at how much land would be needed to feed a population according to a metric like recommended nutrition intake guidelines.

If you think veganism represents a huge shift from the status quo, the Davis proposal represents no less a radical change to a new model, abolishing all animal exploitation including animal farming and fishing, with the sole exception of wholly pasture-raised ruminants. Perhaps this and the actual acceptance of animal rights the position would represent is why people only pay lip service to the proposal.

These crop death arguments are also framed as 'least harm' which is more of a utilitarian calculation than seeing veganism as an anti-exploitation principle. The variable of 'number of animal deaths' is isolated and compared, not the whole impact from use of animals and on the environment, humans and public health. From a rights perspective it is never justified to exploit and slaughter others. We can see this clearly in a human rights context where rights trump any such calculations. Nether the less I think it is valuable to analyse this argument to gain understanding of what it means and how it is used as a reflexive attempt against veganism and how even on its own terms it fails.

It cannot be stressed enough that the Davis model necessitates the abolition of all animal use except for one area of animal use. Is this what people are supporting and practicing? Anyone using the Davis argument should be prepared to have their bluff called, to see if they really are avoiding all seafood. Are they protesting and advocating against fishing? The position that people are committing themselves to must be clearly understood. The Davis proposal is for consuming one grass fed animal per year and the rest of the diet is 100% plant based. All other areas of animal use are avoided also. If they have been so meticulous in their calculation then they can't use that very precise implication to justify any and all animal consumption which just tears up any such calculations and balancing of outcomes. Are they as determined against consumption of pigs, ducks, geese, fish and every other area of animal use (apart from the 'reflexive area') as vegans are?

In the end these attempts to argue from animal rights positions own premises in a reflective way show the strength of the position and the acceptance of its premises. People arguing against veganism have moved or been forced into occupying these areas to make their points against veganism. But by accepting the premises and then having to adhere to the outcomes their arguments backfire and end up strengthening the vegan position. If consuming plants were wrong – it backfires because of land use. If land use itself represents problems through use of human labour or resources and fertiliser, then ecological efficiency again proves that they should be seeking the minimum use of land – the vegan model.

All that is left for the anti-vegan then is to look for extreme exceptions and loopholes

Reflexive Arguments: Part Two

The 'Crop Deaths' argument can be used in a few ways.

1) The Davis Version

First of all they can be used in good faith and with charitable interpretations of positions.
The Steven Davis argument could be interpreted this way as a sincere effort to argue against a vegan position.
The 'Davis version' of the argument is that vegans are responsible for animal deaths too. It asks the question whether some forms of intentional animal use and slaughter that could result in fewer human caused deaths of other animals.
It questions whether our demarcation or criterion for wanting to cause fewer animal deaths should be avoiding animal use or whether this could in fact lead to more deaths due to how some plants are harvested. In that case replacing some type of plant agriculture with animal agriculture would reduce deaths overall. It assumes that the 'go to' position is back to some form of animal use rather than further refining a plant-based diet and swapping some form of plant harvest for another if that was where the initial problem is. Also assumed is that it is wrong to intentionally kill most animals unless intentionally killing one species would prevent the accidental deaths of a greater number of other animals.

2) The Tu Quoque Version

The same argument about crop deaths can be used as Tu Quoque fallacy or whataboutism. They point to problems in a proposed solution but they are used to dismiss potential solutions and so can also be a Nirvana or perfect solution fallacy. The people using the argument in this way have no actual interest in adhering to any consequences that may arise from using the argument.

Although motives can be difficult to determine we can always ask about motives or failing that can look to what people actually practice as a result of their stated positions. When used as a tu quoque version the argument is that 'vegans kill animals too!' and the conclusion can be that it's therefore justifiable to kill any number of animals or any species. They say 'Vegans kill animals too' but the person using it as a tu quoque doesn't actually oppose using or killing any animals in any case. They are actually saying if vegans care about this then they themselves should care about that too. In this use of the argument, they would actually just be satisfied with you answering that you don't care about animal deaths either. This is the real equivalence that they seek if animal deaths are accepted in one form then they are supposedly justified in another. If animal deaths were really a concern then wouldn't be satisfied with no one caring, they would be proactively trying to get people to care and campaigning just as hard as vegans and being against animal deaths in every area as far as the Davis Proposal suggests at the very least.

This version is nothing like the Davis Version because it doesn't adhere to the implications of actually seeking to minimise animal use up to the very specific reflexive point of 'adding some animal use back in' to the model. The

Davis argument could be seen as starting from zero animal use but suggesting adding one area of use creates an overall lower average death toll to animals. The tu quoque version does nothing like this and instead defends the status quo. This is the way the Davis proposal is actually most commonly used as an argument in practice. It is used as a general argument against veganism rather than a very prescriptive version of least harm itself. It is used to argue in favour of indiscriminate consumption of any and all animal products, clearly going against the intention and implications of the Davis Proposal.

3) The Vegan version

A vegan should acknowledge the fact that plant agriculture has many issues and problems currently. (9)
If we frame veganism as 'cruelty free' or not responsible for any harm or death to animals we are sadly mistaken. I think people conflate vegan claims with this claim from companies that market their products as cruelty free, i.e. not tested on animals. We have seen that claims of perfection and purity aren't helpful and are more often used by opponents of veganism (see 'the perfect is the enemy of the good' argument). It leads to Nirvana and perfect solution fallacies.
The vegan position is however that it is still the better position to oppose and avoid all animal use and slaughter as the ideal, even if in practice we can't achieve zero harm to other animals. This is a realistic and practical outlook.
The Davis argument does not hold up due to calculations of numbers of deaths. In analysing the argument, we see that it has isolated the variable of number of deaths and while this is of course a major factor it is by no means the full

picture. There is no equivalence between intentional breeding, confining, transporting, exploiting and slaughtering animals and the accidental deaths of wild animals. Intention does matter in the sense that solutions can be sought within plant agriculture to possibly minimise and even eliminate deaths but this can't be done in animal agriculture where animal slaughter and death is the whole point.

A question I came up with to determine which of the versions of the crop deaths argument people are using is 'which forms of animal use and slaughter are justified by harvest deaths?'

The answers should reveal which position is being adopted. Davis himself would say that the consumption of one grass fed cow per year and being 'vegan' in every other aspect 'apart from this' is the answer.

The confusion or ambivalence of those using it as a tu quoque argument will be revealed in their answer. They don't follow their own advice to vegans, don't have an issue with animal deaths and use it to try and create equivalence between all choices. They are almost as far away from the Davis Proposal themselves as they are from being vegan. You can't pretend to care about accidental wild animal deaths while consuming any sea creatures, fishes or birds, any eggs or pigs, geese, ducks, rabbits, sheep at all! The Davis argument relies on a very specific set of circumstances to work and the force of the argument if it were to succeed would rely on adhering to many of the premises vegans also use, about the value of animal life and minimising animal use and that our choices matter. Anti-vegans are simply not willing to adopt so many of the premises of veganism and take such a gambit. People using the tu quoque version of the argument are not just using a fallacy to dismiss veganism but to dismiss the Davis Proposal itself! They are not interested in minimising animal slaughter.

The Davis version of the crop death argument itself is therefore used to make people comfortable with their current consumption and support for animal use. Imagine if people were actually following their own advice. In this scenario they would be only consuming one animal per year and veganism would be the most harmful practice towards animals in actual existence. Imagine such a world! The Davis argument ends up being a bluff that anti-vegans aren't willing to be called on while they go on supporting almost any and all forms of animal use and slaughter. Perhaps if they realise that the Davis argument is more of a version of 'veganism' rather than a direct opposition to it, they prefer to use crop deaths in a way that creates confusion and obfuscation and paralysis of choice, pretending that all choices are equivalent. Used in this way, the opponents of veganism just want you to despair and maintain the status quo because 'vegans kill animals too!' With the Davis Proposal the variable of number of deaths is the isolated variable. Animal exploitation involves so much more than just the last day of an animal's life on Earth however. Animals are forcibly impregnated, have many forms of procedures such as de-horning and teeth or beak clipping carried out. They live in confinement. Just today as I am writing this I saw two stories of how horrific transporting animals is. (10) (11)
The suffering of these animals that should in no way be being transported is unimaginable. This is just one day. Animals are often stranded for weeks on 'cattle ships'. Lorry crashes with pigs, chickens and sheep are regular

occurrences in the UK. Barn fires that kill thousands of birds are also very common. Due to fears of the spread of diseases, millions of animals have been killed. (12) (13) Then there are the slaughter figures themselves.

In talking numbers it is not the Davis Diet versus a Vegan diet for most people. It is their standard Western Diet versus a vegan diet. Here the numbers are nine billion slaughtered in the United States last year. Approximately 25 million animals are slaughtered each day in the United States. So when people say 'vegans kill animals too' they are arguing from support for this vastly larger number. If they are arguing from a Davis Diet position then they better be adhering to what that actually entails if they are to have any credibility.

The real test of the Davis proposal is to take the implications of it seriously and see what the consequences are. Which proposed model comes out best when all variables such as animal deaths, animal exploitation, the environment, impact on slaughterhouse workers and ecological efficiency are taken into consideration? Then we test to see which version of the argument is being used. Is it a sincere effort to minimise animal use and follow where the results lead? Or is it being used in the tu-quoque sense and resulting in Nirvana fallacies and whataboutisms? Reflexive arguments come in more forms than the crop death argument. I have spent a lot of time analysing it to try and show how the question can be approached in a factual manner and then also how the argument can be used with different intentions. The reflexive arguments are more relevant than others because they identify real issues that shouldn't be dismissed. However, they fail as arguments against veganism because they are used in a fallacious manner when used to argue against veganism. Another way to think about issues is to ask how they are an argument for animal exploitation and slaughter. If anything, reflexive arguments show how we should start from a position of no animal exploitation and slaughter and would arrive at the supposed area that is being argued for in the reflexive argument more economically than arguing from or for the status quo of unrestricted and ubiquitous animal use.

Plants tho
In terms of food waste we find that animal agriculture has food waste built in to its very nature. This is due to trophic level consumption.

Food Waste - ''Almost half of harvested crops – or 2.1 billion tonnes – are lost through over-consumption, consumer waste and inefficiencies in production processes. Livestock production is the least efficient process, with losses of 78 per cent or 840 million tonnes. Some 1.08 billion tonnes of harvested crops are used to produce 240 million tonnes of edible animal products including meat, milk and eggs. This stage alone accounts for 40 per cent of all losses of harvested crops.'' ''Increased demand for some foods, particularly meat and dairy products, would decrease the efficiency of the food system and could make it difficult to feed the world's expanding population in sustainable ways. Meeting this demand could cause environmental harm by increasing greenhouse gas emissions, depleting water supplies and causing loss of biodiversity.
Encouraging people to eat fewer animal products, reduce waste and not exceed their nutritional needs could help to reverse these trends'' (14)

This shows how funnelling food through animals is systemic food waste. Anyone concerned about 'harvest deaths' should be avoiding this most egregious form of food waste.

Hannah Ritchie writing on Our World In Data states ''Livestock takes up nearly 80% of global agricultural land, yet produces less than 20% of the world's supply of calories. This means that what we eat is more important than how much we eat in determining the amount of land required to produce our food. As we get richer, our diets tend to diversify and per capita meat consumption rises; economic development unfortunately exerts an increasing impact on land resources.''

Feed conversion ratios

If humans were farmed and slaughtered by an alien species it would be obvious to us that we were being kept alive by being fed and that the resultant 'food' from one of our bodies is much less than the amount we would have eaten ourselves. The same is true for other animals. The conversion of feed into 'meat' is the Feed Conversion ratio and this varies between species as each have general body weight and lifespans. (15) Of course, animals in the canned hunting system of animal agriculture are only kept alive and fed for the minimum time that they can reach the maximum weight – this is their 'slaughter weight'. The younger the better for animal farmers and animal consumers.

Ecological Efficiency

In comparing the cultivation of animals versus plants, there is a clear difference in magnitude of energy efficiency.

Edible kilocalories produced from kilocalories of energy required for cultivation are: 18.1% for chicken, 6.7% for grass-fed beef, 5.7% for farmed salmon, and 0.9% for shrimp. In contrast, potatoes yield 123%, corn produce 250%, and soy results in 415% of input calories converted to calories able to be utilized by humans. This disparity in efficiency reflects the reduction in production from moving up trophic levels. Thus, it is more energetically efficient to form a diet from lower trophic levels. (16)

Here we see the efficiency of 6.7% for grass-fed beef being amongst the worst feed conversion ratios compared to the amount of calories that can be produced from land growing plant foods.

Here you can also see how much protein can be obtained from land.

'Soybeans produce at least two times more usable protein per unit area than any other major vegetable or grain crop, except for hemp which can produce up to 33 g/m2(290 lb/acre). They produce 5 to 10 times more protein per unit area than land set aside for grazing animals to make milk, and up to 15 times more protein per unit area than land set aside for meat production.'' (17)

On the subject of soy, many anti-vegans will switch the argument to deforestation and again the argument backfires. 'About 85 percent of the world's soybeans are processed, or "crushed," annually into soybean meal and oil. Approximately 98 percent of the soybean meal that is crushed is further processed into animal feed with the balance used to make soy flour and proteins. Of the oil fraction, 95 percent is consumed as edible oil; the rest is used for industrial products such as fatty acids, soaps and biodiesel. Soy is one of the few plants that provides a complete protein as it contains all eight amino acids essential for human health.' (18)

Ecological efficiency favours veganism and counters anti-vegan arguments about loss of biodiversity, deaths of animals as a result of harvesting plants, use of resources, transport etc because a plant-based diet uses the least land and it therefore follows that these other issues raised are also lessened correspondingly or worsened by animal agriculture that uses more plant agriculture plus exploits and slaughters trillions of animals annually on top of this.

'Regenerative agriculture' of the type at White Oaks Pasture takes up 2.5 times more land and so even according to Davis' calculations this ideal model version still kills more animals in pasture -'Davis estimates that 15 wild animals per hectare per year are killed as a result of harvesting annual crops, and guesses that maybe half that, or 7.5 animals per hectare per year, are killed on grazed land with managed perennial forage.' (19)

 Lamey writes in the notes to his piece about this argument about further refinement of the feed ratio and ecological efficiency of land use for plants or for animal agriculture (animal agriculture includes vast amounts of plant agriculture!) -
''Gaverick Matheny, "Least Harm: A Defense of Vegetarianism from Davis's Omnivorous Proposal - Matheny suggests in personal communication that cropland may in fact be even more productive than he originally estimated. At the outer limit, he writes, land devoted to grazing cattle in a cold climate is sixty-seven times less

productive than land devoted to soy crops. Matheny's revised estimate is based on a soybean crop yield of thirty-seven bushels per acre, with an average meal yield of forty-eight lbs per bushel, of which forty-eight percent is protein. That works out to 852 lbs protein per acre or 955 kg protein per hectare. Grazing cows, by contrast, gain an average of 131 kg per hectare, with an average 0.42 kg of meat per kilogram of live weight, and 0.26 kg of protein per kilogram of meat. That works out to 14.3 kg of protein per hectare or one sixty-seventh the amount produced from soy. As Matheny notes, pasture-finished cattle might have a different total efficiency, and grass-fed cows in a hotter climate could be considerably more productive. Nonetheless, he believes his revised figures are more representative than those in "Least Harm." For the purposes of rebutting Davis, the difference between Matheny's 1:10 and 1:67 ratios is academic, so I have continued to use the 1:10 figure in the main text. Given Davis's estimates regarding the number of animals killed in beef and crop farming, anything above a 1:2 ratio invalidates his argument."

In other words even if the ratio of efficiency for the pasture based model may be as much as 67 to 1 and all that is required for the reflexive Davis argument to once again backfire is that there is a 2 to 1 ratio of efficiency in favour of plant agriculture. Given the ten percent law of trophic level energy transfer it seems reasonable to me to take 10:1 as a good average of plant agriculture efficiency to animal agriculture efficiency in general. Different crops especially legumes give greater efficiencies and have other benefits like fixing nitrogen in soil and being more versatile foodstuffs.

Ten percent law

In the ten percent law of transfer of energy from one trophic level to the next higher level, only about ten percent of the transferred energy is available to the next stage with the rest being lost to the environment through heat transfer, respiration and other processes. In other words, because we are dealing with living animals the process of them living takes up the vast amount of energy used and the output of energy available in the animal's flesh is always going to be a lot less than the energy used in the biological process of living.

It should not surprise us then when we see figures that say animal based foods use up to ten times the amount of natural resources compared to plant agriculture. Any loss of energy is multiplied by ten as we move up to the next trophic level.

The food chain

''When organisms are consumed, 10% of the energy in the food is fixed into their flesh and is available for next trophic level (carnivores or omnivores). When a carnivore or an omnivore consumes that animal, only about 10% of energy is fixed in its flesh for the higher level.

The ten percent law provides a basic understanding on the cycling of food chains. Furthermore, the ten percent law shows the inefficiency of energy capture at each successive trophic level. The rational conclusion is that energy efficiency is best preserved by sourcing food as close to the initial energy source as possible.'' (20)

You can't simultaneously boast of being 'top of the food chain' and using fewer resources. Being top of a chain of animal exploitation and slaughter means you are multiplying your impact the higher on that chain you think you are.

In reality though, humans rank around the same level as pigs and anchovies. (21) This is not a boast you will see from people who always flatter themselves with comparisons to lions and not one of the most misunderstood and maligned of animals, pigs. Most animals live in balance with their environment and other species. Invoking a 'food chain' hierarchy with humans at the top is the height of hubris. Humans fancy themselves as apex predators. Apex predators keep their numbers in check and that number can only be small in relation to the number of animals they prey on. With billions of humans wanting to be predators the number of animals they eat must be even larger, but artificially so beyond any dynamic that would be found in a healthy ecosystem. (22)

In truth, humans are more like kleptoparasites and out of control canned hunters rather than 'apex predators'. Kleptoparasites steal their food from other animals. It is ironic that one of the jokes used against vegans 'why do you steal the animal's food if you like them so much?' more fittingly applies to those who consume other animal's milks. The next time someone says that just ask them if they consume dairy.

Humans have had a direct impact on many species and driven them to extinction through hunting. Only the artificial canned hunting operation of today's 'animal agriculture' can sustain this hunting culture in terms of sheer numbers. It has nothing to do with 'balance' of ecosystems and is in fact quite the opposite. (23)

Greenhouse Gases

In terms of GHG emissions the Davis Proposal has the downside of increasing these due to ruminant animal population and increasing deforestation. 'Cattle ranching is the largest driver of deforestation in every Amazon country, accounting for 80% of current deforestation rates. Amazon Brazil is home to approximately 200 million head of cattle, and is the largest exporter in the world, supplying about one quarter of the global market.' (24) These animals are grass fed on fresh pasture that used to be the Amazon rainforest. Cattle have replaced nearly twice as much forest as all the other commodities listed here - Oil Palm, Soy, Cocoa, Plantation rubber, Coffee Plantation wood fibre. ''Globally, the conversion of forests to cattle pasture resulted in an estimated 45.1 Mha of deforestation between 2001 and 2015, five times more than for any of the other analyzed commodities.'' (see note 24) A Davis model calls for more deforestation and conversion to pasture unless it is only meant for a small percentage of humanity.

Alternatively ''Global farmland use could be reduced by more than 75% – an area equivalent to the US, China, European Union and Australia combined – and still feed the world. Biggest analysis to date reveals huge footprint of livestock – it provides just 18% of calories but takes up 83% of farmland. Other recent research shows 86% of all land mammals are now livestock or humans. The scientists also found that even the very lowest impact meat and dairy products still cause much more environmental harm than the least sustainable vegetable and cereal growing.''

Damian Carrington Environment editor, The Guardian, Thu 31 May 2018 (via Global Catholic Climate Movement)

There is much more opportunity for sequestering carbon and not increasing methane production in the vegan model. Studies have looked at the opportunity for less land use and how rewilding can sequester carbon better than other models. (25) In fact only a vegan model results in zero further deforestation while still being able to feed the world population. (26)

''Beef requires 20 times more land and emits 20 times more GHG emissions per gram of edible protein than common plant proteins, such as beans. And while the majority of the world's grasslands cannot grow crops or trees, such "native grasslands" are already heavily used for livestock production, meaning additional beef demand will likely increase pressure on forests.'' (27)
Shifting the US back to exclusively grass-fed beef production would require up to 270% more land if Americans did not reduce their consumption. (28)

The key takeaway is that any issues pointed to in plant agriculture are only magnified exponentially if you are using more plant agriculture to feed animals who are fed and slaughtered. (29)

Part Three: Conclusion

I do take the emergence of more reflexive arguments as a positive sign. Whereas most arguments against veganism are irrelevant, these at least have more relevance. Their strength however is borrowed from vegan arguments and premises which they use to try to create a reflexive argument.
When we look at Graham's Hierarchy of disagreement we see that the better quality arguments are those that are increasingly to the point and therefore relevant. Moving up a hierarchy of quality we go from arguments that fail to address the opponent's argument and instead attack them or use other fallacies and diversions and as we move up the hierarchy to better arguments they address the actual argument with valid points, sound reasoning and evidence. Applying this to vegan arguments we can use Graham's hierarchy to filter out and disqualify the lower quality arguments that are irrelevant or fallacies. What we are left with then are better arguments that at least attempt to address the issues and the vegan premises. With the Reflexive arguments we see that this is exactly what's happening. They may still not be successful in arguing against veganism but they are at least more relevant.

It could be said that vegans look for morally relevant similarities in order not to exploit and slaughter animals whereas non-vegans look for irrelevant differences in order to do just that and justify it. If we keep the principle of relevance in mind it can help filter out many irrelevant arguments but also give us clues to what the relevant answer would be. In trying to build a fairer and more equitable society it is also how we determine what is morally relevant and how irrelevant factors are used to discriminate.

Anti-vegans want arguments to be in less relevant areas so they don't have to adhere to the implications of a reflexive argument. The character of certain individual vegans, certain types of vegan advocacy and analogies they don't like. All are irrelevant to the core principles of veganism and avoiding animal exploitation. A good question to ask is 'Is this your argument against veganism?' or ask yourself 'is this the real reason why I support animal use and slaughter?'

Loopholes and exceptions that prove the rule

Realising this, those arguing for animal use and or slaughter try to argue that they eliminate the usual chain of production.

This is an attempt to 'short circuit' the usual processes of energy transfer through trophic levels which multiplies the energy loss. The better-quality arguments are better precisely because they are more relevant and address the points. To try and form a better argument against veganism people are forced into the areas that use reflexive arguments. These positions accept the vegan premises and principles and in trying to argue against veganism end up only being able to try and find exceptions that prove the rule or loopholes that short circuit the normal way animal products are sourced.

If the animal they slaughter and eat has not had any harvested food fed to them then these links in the chain are cut out. The animal is supposedly only eating what is on the land they live on.

Other ways to 'short circuit' are if animals are fed food waste or if you are consuming animals or animal products outside of systems of production. These can be things like being a freegan, hunting or foraging for your own animals, consuming roadkill and begging, borrowing or stealing, as long as the usual trophic level transfer system is circumvented. This is a sign of the strength of the vegan position. Look at the positions people have to adopt to argue against it. They are forced to invent extreme hypotheticals to lay traps and gotchas and put vegans in no-win scenarios. It is important to understand what positions your own arguments commit you to. It may be that you have found an extremely rare exception but paradoxically the logic of the exception can only exist if the rest of the system is valid or it is nonsensical. Better arguments move from outright denial of animal sentience and individual responsibility to acceptance of these principles and along a scale of veganism being extreme and too much to veganism not being enough!

Advocating for any of these things means that the position being taken is to avoid any products from systems of production. It accepts the arguments of ecological efficiency but seeks to operate outside systems that are subject to those constraints.

Consuming roadkill is another option for short circuiting. If people are stealing eggs or honey from animals then any found or stolen items also qualify in this area.

Vegans face a more difficult task arguing against these areas and it is the anti-vegans here that will be trying to tell vegans that they should be doing these things because they would also cut out systems of production. So is freeganism more morally advanced than veganism? Is fruitarianism also? Obviously being able to completely grow and/or forage your own plant foods would be the ideal.

I don't think we as vegans should get too defensive in these areas. Are we reacting like a vegetarian does when told something is more moral in that they should avoid the exploitation and slaughter of egg and dairy production?

I advocate veganism because it is practical and I can advise on the practical aspects of working a 9-5 job, having a family and wide variety of commitments, living in society and being vegan.

Vegans are not asking anyone to do anything they do not do themselves.

If anti-vegans want to try to call vegan's bluff and say we should be doing more where is the commitment from them to adhere to actually avoiding the system of animal agriculture? What is their practical advice? Imagine a world where veganism was the least moral way of life according to these critics. Imagine how many forms of animal use and slaughter this would have eliminated. When you realise this you realise how many of what I would call the 'vegan premises' are actually accepted by people trying to argue against veganism this way.

You are accepting it is better to have less animal suffering and killing. You are accepting animal sentience. You are accepting ecological efficiency and that it is better to be more efficient and so on. They are accepting the premises but reaching different conclusions.

I only feel comfortable advocating something I do myself, taking into consideration the fact I work full time and have family commitments. So I don't expect others to do anything I'm not willing to do myself. I think the challenge to grow more of your own food is a good one. It's another way to cut out the systems of production. However, you can't argue about veganism being a privilege and then seriously demand that people invest time and effort into growing their own food. If people can then good for them but I don't demand a higher level of self-sufficiency than I can reasonably achieve when advocating to people in a similar situation to myself.

These sort of issues are probably the strongest attempt to argue against veganism on its own terms. But this is where it becomes an issue of integrity and honesty for those arguing in such away. The problem for anti-vegans is that it is on veganism's own terms. You are accepting that so many areas vegans avoid should be avoided by you too. By arguing in this way you aren't arguing that nothing should be done.

In reality most of the time it is amoral equivalence argument.

People using the argument have no honest intention of avoiding systemic production of animal products, just like they don't only buy 'humane' animal products etc.

They are playing Devil's Advocate for the position with no intention of adhering to it. When their bluff is called they say they don't really care to follow their own advice. To save going round the houses maybe we should ask them whether they follow their own advice first.

The problem with other proposed solutions is that they can't be scaled up from individuals to populations.

Consider the following proposals scaled up to meet the demand of the human population -

Hunting – 7 billion plus hunters

Foraging and freeganism – 7 billion plus dumpster divers

Grass fed –the land requirements are more than is available on Earth. The Amazon rainforest is being converted to pasture for grazing as it is.

Anti-vegan arguments can also be argued against in a reflexive manner. The 3 R's of animal research are meant to provide a framework for 'more humane animal use' in medical research settings. They are
Replacement, Reduction and Refinement. But why stop there? If we should minimise animal use why not replace animal-based foods with plant-based foods and reduce animal use to the minimum possible?

I find that those who promote so called 'ethical omnivore movement' are unwilling to state what sort of cap they think should be put on animal product consumption which makes me suspicious that they aren't actually interested in advocating such a thing but rather want to be the equivalent of a 'halo product' that greenwashes the sector and makes everyone more comfortable with meat and dairy consumption overall.

The Halo effect is something utilised by advertisers and manufacturers to give a positive impression in one area that they hope will be transferred to other areas. Car manufacturers for example will make limited runs of high performance vehicles that serve as halo cars and bring prestige to the brand as a whole. The idea that some animal products that come from very limited and specific forms of production are ethical is used as a halo effect to legitimise and justify the rest of the sector. This is what we see with the idea that some forms of slaughter are 'humane' or that confining and killing animals is 'ethical'. People don't actually limit themselves to these practices or condemn the unethical areas with anywhere near the same energy they reserve for criticising vegans. 'Ethical Butchers' that sell these 'halo products' also sell numerous other animal products that don't meet their ethical criteria and they are happy to promote general consumption of meat and dairy whatever the source. If there is an 'ethical omnivore movement' doesn't that imply that by default all other practices not covered by them are 'unethical'? Have you ever seen them arguing with people who consume animal products from what by their own definition should be the 'unethical omnivorism'? Or do they just argue with vegans?

Trade-offs

A trade-off is a situation where as one thing increases another will decrease and vice versa. One quality is exchanged for another but there must be some loss to that quality in order to gain another.

In terms of animal agriculture trade-offs exist within the system when greater 'welfare' is proposed through less intensive farming methods – the trade-off here is that consumption levels would have to be capped at certain levels or only a certain percentage of a population could be fed from such sources. In terms of the harvest deaths argument the trade-off comes from having to consume one and only one, animal product that you think lessens the overall death count. Consuming any more than this constitutes a trade-off. There are environmental trade-offs where it is proposed that as beef and lamb are worse in terms of greenhouse emissions it is better to consume chickens that have a lower environmental footprint. However the trade-off is for worse animal welfare from more intensive systems and higher death counts compared to larger mammals. The trade-off for trying to feed more people with holistic grazing or regenerative practices from no longer using more land is intensification making welfare concerns and numbers of animal deaths once again more prominent.

Lies by Omission

Of course all these trade-offs within animal agriculture can be avoided in a vegan model. Trade-offs exist within plant agriculture too but as discussed previously, once the biggest levers of avoiding meat and dairy are pulled then the choices within veganism can be further refined to ever greater levels. (30) (31) (32)

A 'lie by omission' is an instance of not telling the whole truth, leaving out important facts that could affect a conclusion and failing to correct any misconceptions by providing the full facts.

As Lorelei Plotczyk of Truth or Drought says in the article on marginal land previously discussed, the omission comes from not making it clear that not every bit of land needs to be used and that plant foods can actually be grown on the land. Essentially all comparisons and trade-offs are implied to be required within animal exploitation systems. They omit mentioning a comparison to vegan models where the whole of animal agriculture would come off worse in comparison. It's worth trying to see if there is a bigger picture we are missing. As in the case of 'humane slaughter' we are exposed to many false dilemmas when in fact there are often other options.

If no forms of animal exploitation and slaughter existed, which ones would you introduce to the world and why?

If you were designing a new agricultural system from scratch to be the most efficient and involve the least animal slaughter, what would it look like?

The point of these questions is to show that starting with a vegan model should be the default. The Davis proposal and models like that suggest reflexively adding some forms as a trade-off for overall numbers of animal deaths. When people have their bluff called on whether this is what they actually follow themselves it is clear how far they actually are from the starting point of the vegan model. Taking these reflexive arguments at face value and on their own terms they still fail at demonstrating that veganism is not the best option. From an animal rights perspective they are utilitarian calculations but even on this score they fail.

Concerned about harvest deaths? There would be fewer if so many straw man arguments weren't used.

'About 2,000 pounds of grains must be supplied to livestock in order to produce enough meat and other livestock products to support a person for a year, whereas 400 pounds of grain eaten directly will support a person for a year. Thus, a given quantity of grain eaten directly will feed 5 times as many people as it will if it is eaten indirectly by humans in the form of livestock products.'
- Marion Eugene Ensminger (American Society of Animal Science)

The harvest deaths argument is just one example of a reflexive argument against veganism. They try to take on veganism on its own terms but those very terms end up backfiring with greater force and making a case for veganism.

Recommended reading –

https://freefromharm.org/common-justifications-for-eating-animals/comparing-animal-deaths-production-plant-animal-foods/

https://www.theflamingvegan.com/view-post/Vegan-Mythbusting-1-Are-wild-animals-killed-when-grain-is-harvested-for-vegans

https://uvearchives.wordpress.com/2008/01/01/contrasting-harms-vegan-agriculture-versus-animal-agriculture/

https://freefromharm.org/common-justifications-for-eating-animals/why-plant-crops-dont-kill-more-wildlife-than-pasture-raised-animals/

https://anupamkatkar.com/2015/10/08/debunking-cultivating-crops-for-vegans-kills-more-animals-than-pasture-grazing-livestock/

https://medium.com/age-of-awareness/no-vegans-dont-kill-more-animals-than-human-omnivores-a1975d1a497c

Notes to Chapter Six

(1) Davis, Steven L. "The Least Harm Principle May Require That Humans Consume a Diet Containing Large Herbivores, Not a Vegan Diet," Journal of Agricultural and Environmental Ethics 16, no. 4 (2003): 387-394.
(2) https://www.greenqueen.com.hk/from-chicken-to-mushrooms-livestock-farmers-transitioning-to-sustainable-options/
(3) https://www.animalvisuals.org/projects/data/1mc
(4) https://www.theguardian.com/world/2014/apr/25/german-drones-protect-young-deer-combine-harvesters
(5) See for example https://vectorbirds.com/en/services/commissioned-flights/fawn-search-and-rescue-with-drone-and-infrared-camera?fbclid=IwAR062FYodsDdb8xLVdSH4h1cI7Q_NmEUaEz6FtU8YIo_YgrQmQTaw3kbReY
(6) Matheny, Gaverick. "Least Harm: A Defense of Vegetarianism From Steven Davis's Omnivorous Proposal," Journal of Agricultural and Environmental Ethics 16 (2003): 505-511.
(7) Lamey, Andy. "Food Fight! Davis versus Regan on the Ethics of Eating Beef," Journal of Social Philosophy 38, no. 2 (2007): 331-348
(8) https://uvearchives.wordpress.com/tag/contrasting-harms/
(9) https://arzone.ning.com/forum/topics/intention-does-matter-benny-malone
(10) https://www.bbc.co.uk/news/world-asia-54008087
(11) https://www.shropshirestar.com/news/local-hubs/bridgnorth/2020/09/02/lorry-with-400-sheep-involved-in-crash/
(12) http://www.countinganimals.com/is-vegan-outreach-right-about-how-many-animals-suffer-to-death/
(13) https://inews.co.uk/news/uk/dead-arrival-million-chickens-die-reaching-slaughterhouse-119364
(14) Fifth of world's food lost to over-eating and waste, study finds https://www.sciencedaily.com/releases/2017/02/170221101024.htm University of York - https://www.york.ac.uk/news-and-events/news/2017/research/over-eating-food-waste/
(15) https://awellfedworld.org/feed-ratios/
(16) Eshel, Gidon and Martin, Pamela A. Diet, Energy, and Global Warming. Earth Interactions. 2005. 10: 1- 17

(17) https://en.wikipedia.org/wiki/Edible_protein_per_unit_area_of_land

(18) SoyFacts - http://www.soyatech.com/soy_facts.htm
(19) White Oaks - Ecosystem Impacts and Productive Capacity of a Multi-Species Pastured Livestock System
https://www.frontiersin.org/articles/10.3389/fsufs.2020.544984/full#F2
(20) https://en.wikipedia.org/wiki/Ecological_efficiency
https://ourworldindata.org/agricultural-land-by-global-diets
(21) https://www.smithsonianmag.com/science-nature/where-do-humans-really-rank-on-the-food-chain-180948053/
Trophic levels of humans - https://molcyt.org/2013/12/05/from-vegan-to-meat-human-diet-and-trophic-levels/
Trophic Levels https://www.sciencedaily.com/releases/2019/02/190206101055.
(22) htmhttps://www.livescience.com/first-human-caused-animal-extinction.html
(23) Biomass - https://www.ecowatch.com/biomass-humans-animals-2571413930.html   Land Mammal Biomass - https://xkcd.com/1338/
(24) https://globalforestatlas.yale.edu/amazon/land-use/cattle-ranching
https://www.bloomberg.com/news/features/2020-12-17/saving-the-amazon-starts-with-cleaning-up-the-beef-industry?fbclid=IwAR1VguHcPqGnrpsnZ1648u7mtcKMsCMG0TAgsmdKIpitxw4ELRQFvTrYUdQ
(25) The carbon opportunity cost of animal-sourced food production on land   https://www.nature.com/articles/s41893-020-00603-4
(26) Feeding the world without further deforestation is possible
https://www.sciencedaily.com/releases/2016/04/160419120147.html
https://www.wri.org/blog/2019/04/6-pressing-questions-about-beef-and-climate-change-answered
(27) https://www.wri.org/blog/2019/04/6-pressing-questions-about-beef-and-climate-change-answered
(28) https://www.linkedin.com/pulse/free-range-isnt-free-matthew-hayek/
https://www.theguardian.com/environment/2020/dec/23/organic-meat-production-just-as-bad-for-climate-study-finds
(29) https://ourworldindata.org/environmental-impacts-of-food
https://www.pnas.org/content/115/25/6506
(30) https://www.theguardian.com/environment/2018/may/31/avoiding-meat-and-dairy-is-single-biggest-way-to-reduce-your-impact-on-earth

(31) https://faunalytics.org/reducing-environmental-impacts-food-consumer-producer-leverage-points/
(32) https://www.grain.org/article/entries/5976-emissions-impossible-how-big-meat-and-dairy-are-heating-up-the-planet
https://www.theguardian.com/environment/2020/dec/23/organic-meat-production-just-as-bad-for-climate-study-finds

Chapter Seven

The Last Time I Lost an Argument I Went Vegan

The scientific consensus is overwhelmingly on the side of veganism in terms of animal sentience being established, the health of vegan diets and the environmental cost of animal agriculture.

Animal sentience

As Marc Bekoff writes 'Scientists have ample, detailed, empirical facts to declare that nonhuman animals are sentient beings, and with each study, there are fewer and fewer skeptics.' [1] [2]

The Cambridge Declaration on Consciousness

"The absence of a neocortex does not appear to preclude an organism from experiencing affective states. Convergent evidence indicates that non-human animals have the neuroanatomical, neurochemical, and neurophysiological substrates of conscious states along with the capacity to exhibit intentional behaviors. Consequently, the weight of evidence indicates that humans are not unique in possessing the neurological substrates that generate consciousness. Nonhuman animals, including all mammals and birds, and many other creatures, including octopuses, also possess these neurological substrates." [3]

Zoonotic Pandemics

I would go vegan but I could never give up pandemics.

When I read Guns, Germs, and Steel by Jared Diamond I discovered the following - 'living in close proximity to livestock resulted in widespread transmission of diseases, including from animals to humans. Smallpox, measles, and influenza were the result of close proximity between dense populations of animals and humans.' I have written this book during the Covid-19 pandemic and while it is not yet definitively proven what the origin was it seems highly probable that it is zoonotic in nature and has transferred from an animal host to infect humans. A list of zoonotic diseases includes all major pandemics so it would be an extreme outlier for a virus like Covid-19 not to have arisen from animals. (4) (5) (6)

Antibiotic resistance also represents a major threat to public health.
'The high volume of antibiotics in food-producing animals contributes to the development of antimicrobial-resistant bacteria, particularly in settings of intensive animal production. In some countries, the total amount of antibiotics used in animals is 4 times larger than the amount used in humans. In many countries much of the antibiotics used in animals are for growth promotion and prevention of disease, not to treat sick animals.
These bacteria can be transmitted from animals to humans via direct contact between animals and humans, or through the food chain and the environment. Antimicrobial-resistant infections in humans can cause longer illnesses, increased frequency of hospitalization, and treatment failures that can result in death. Some types of bacteria that cause serious infections in humans have already developed resistance to most or all of the available treatments and we

are running out of treatment options for some types of infection. WHO recommends an overall reduction in use of antibiotics in food-producing animals to help preserve their effectiveness for human medicine.' (7)

Health

'It is the position of the Academy of Nutrition and Dietetics that appropriately planned vegetarian**, *including vegan***, diets are healthful, nutritionally adequate, and may provide health benefits for the prevention and treatment of certain diseases. These diets are appropriate for all stages of the life cycle, including pregnancy, lactation, infancy, childhood, adolescence, older adulthood, and for athletes. Plant-based diets are more environmentally sustainable than diets rich in animal products because they use fewer natural resources and are associated with much less environmental damage. Vegetarians and vegans are at reduced risk of certain health conditions, including ischemic heart disease, type 2 diabetes, hypertension, certain types of cancer, and obesity. Low intake of saturated fat and high intakes of vegetables, fruits, whole grains, legumes, soy products, nuts, and seeds (all rich in fiber and phytochemicals) are characteristics of vegetarian and vegan diets that produce lower total and low-density lipoprotein cholesterol levels and better serum glucose control. These factors contribute to reduction of chronic disease. Vegans need reliable sources of vitamin B-12, such as fortified foods or supplements.' (8)
For advice on healthy plant-based diets I recommend vegan registered dieticians like Ginny Messina and her site The Vegan R.D. and books like Vegan For Life. For the purposes of an ethical argument it is sufficient that we can be at least as healthy and fit on a vegan diet. It is vital to

supplement B-12 and the best advice on this can be found in the aforementioned resources.

Environment

The same is true for an ethical argument for veganism as far as the environment goes. If veganism was significantly worse for the environment or impossible due to an absolute necessity for animal inputs then that necessity would cancel out essential areas from ethical scrutiny as we would have no choice. The fact is that veganism reduces our impact on the environment as we have seen in many studies. We have seen that the main reason for this is the trophic level we eat from and how eating as low as possible as a general rule will yield greater efficiency than consuming animals and cycling our nutrients through other animals first with all the loss of energy that this represents. Any arguments levelled against veganism about its impact have to contend with this ecological efficiency. This is the reason most arguments against veganism backfire, and in an exponential way at that.
'Across studies, consistent evidence indicated that a dietary pattern higher in plant-based foods (e.g., vegetables, fruits, legumes, seeds, nuts, whole grains) and lower in animal-based foods (especially red meat), as well as lower in total energy, is both healthier and associated with a lesser impact on the environment.' (9)

Phosphorus use and supply is a neglected issue but should be a major concern for the future.
'The risks of peak phosphorus can be countered with some simple solutions. Eating less meat is a start as huge amounts are used to rear livestock for meat. The chances are that agricultural yields are limited by phosphorus availability and will be further stretched as the global population grows.' (10)

'Fertiliser use has quadrupled over the past half century and will continue rising as the population expands. The growing wealth of developing countries allows people to afford more meat which has a "phosphorus footprint" 50 times higher than most vegetables. This, together with the increasing usage of biofuels, is estimated to double the demand for phosphorus fertilisers by 2050.' (11)

'Soil nutrients in grasslands are removed through withdrawal in these livestock products and through animal manure that originates from grasslands and is spread in croplands. This leads to loss of soil fertility, because globally most grasslands receive no mineral fertilizer. Here we show that phosphorus (P) inputs (mineral and organic) in global grasslands will have to increase more than fourfold in 2050 relative to 2005 to achieve an anticipated 80% increase in grass production (for milk and meat), while maintaining the soil P status. Combined with requirements for cropland, we estimate that mineral P fertilizer use must double by 2050 to sustain future crop and grassland production.' (12)

Hypocrisy or Consistency.

'The advantage of a reform in diet, is obviously greater than that of any other. It strikes at the root of the evil. To remedy the abuses of legislation, before we annihilate the propensities by which they are produced, is to suppose, that by taking away the effect, the cause will cease to operate. But the efficacy of this system depends entirely on the proselytism of individuals, and grounds its merits as a benefit to the community, upon the total change of the dietetic habits in its members. It proceeds securely from a number of particular cases, to one that is universal, and has this advantage over the contrary mode, that one error does not invalidate all

that has gone before.'

A Vindication of Natural Diet
by Percy Bysshe Shelley   London, 1813 (13)

Not every statement needs to be argued against. Lots of things should be acknowledged but we can simply ask how they are an argument in support of exploiting and slaughtering animals or against veganism.
I don't call people 'hypocrites' as I think it is a word that is seen as an insult.
Those who limit the scope of veganism to argue against adopting plant-based diets still do not take the opportunity to argue against speciesism or against animal use quite apart from any ability to adhere to a plant based diet personally. They are hostile to vegans and don't support their arguments and fail to address speciesism, even if for some medical reason they can't follow a plant based diet.

Some people who use a form of tu-quoque argumentation argue that vegans should minimise harm through only consuming what is absolutely necessary and sufficient to sustain themselves. If vegans use a 'necessity' argument then this is a natural rebuttal. The necessity argument states that causing unnecessary harm to animals is wrong. Animal products cause harm to animals. Consuming animal products is unnecessary. Therefore consuming animal products causes unnecessary harm to animals. It's understandable that anti-vegans would try and turn this argument round or extend it to plant products using the same formula. Reframing the argument in terms of animal use and explaining that the necessity part is only what enables veganism, but is not the main argument itself can help. However some anti-vegans are persistent in this line of questioning and will demand vegans should calorie restrict 'if they were serious'. If vegans did actually advocate this do you think these anti-vegans would be happy about that? It is a no-win situation. If we advocate for an unrestrictive and easier to adopt lifestyle they will say veganism doesn't go far enough. If we advocated such strictures they would say it promotes unhealthy dietary restrictions and eating disorders. I think these things are best left to the individual vegan to decide their own plant-based diet. There is always room for improvement but if veganism is to be normalised then starting with such 'advice' from anti-vegans who don't follow it doesn't help the movement. This is one example of a 'Schrodinger's joke' – where the person says something and depending on your response might say they were serious or just joking. Anti-vegans may put you in similar no-win situations where whatever your answer is they will argue that the opposite is the real solution. As you can't win this game, don't play it and try to pin any snipers down. Or if you do provide an answer you can only try to explain why the other option would not be viable or is not what you can advocate with any integrity.

Dealing with difficult VEGANS!

It might happen that you are on social media advocating for veganism and there is an antagonistic reply about self-righteousness or preaching. After some back and forth you may find out that this person is actually vegan. They have taken issue with how you are advocating for veganism or perhaps even the fact that you are advocating for it at all. They usually support advocating for Reducetarianism themselves or something else like vegetarianism or only avoiding eating chickens. They might not believe in promoting veganism and aren't advocating for it themselves. They may start using arguments about how you shouldn't be advocating because

you are a hypocrite and so in no position to 'judge' or 'preach'.
You can ask them why they don't seem to want you to be advocating for veganism rather than continually defending your right to do so. Already the tone has been set that merely advocating veganism is preachy even if you are doing your best to advocate well. Arguments about you being a hypocrite are often designed to silence you and stop you advocating. In calling everyone hypocrites it sets up a sort of atmosphere of negativity about anyone advocating for something. Environmentalists as well as vegans are subject to being called hypocrites in an attempt to silence them.

What a lot of people are trying to do is 'give you a taste of your own medicine' and turn judgement and accusations of hypocrisy back on to you. These tu-quoque arguments may happen without provocation or in response to any actual 'judgemental' behaviour on your part. It's a manifestation of the anticipated moral reproach we examined in chapter three and a case of getting a pre-emptive strike in.

I think it is much better to talk about **consistency rather than hypocrisy**. For one thing the word hypocrisy will be seen as an insult and a personal attack. If we turn it round to talking about how we can all work on being more consistent with our ethics it is a more positive framing. It is then a matter of us all working on self-improvement and being morally consistent rather than tearing each other down.
A familiar question animal rights activists face, or used to at least, if they are protesting on the streets is 'are those leather shoes?' which is an attempt to call them hypocrites (and also unlikely considering they are probably vegan). What if we see it as a call for consistency however? What if it a genuine recognition that in order to be more

consistent they should not wear animal skins and similarly if they don't eat meat then they should also not consume dairy or eggs? Rather than being a 'gotcha' for vegans this actually strengthens the case and shows they are being more consistent.

Where to draw the line on consistency.

Critics of veganism will be unlikely to stop there however and if they are aware of how far a vegan already goes in their consistency they will demand even more in other areas besides animal use. This is moving beyond the scope of veganism itself but animals may still be affected through wild animal suffering and the environment so the points are valid and we shouldn't be defensive when they are raised. The difference lies in the fact that vegans are advocating veganism while actually following their own advice. **Vegans aren't asking anyone to do anything they aren't doing themselves or beyond reasonable levels of achievability**. Vegans recognise people have jobs and family commitments and the change to a vegan lifestyle shouldn't change these dramatically for most people. However when consistency or rather hypocrisy arguments are used in a hyper-critical way they make bigger demands of the vegan and are not usually followed by the person themselves. The anti-vegan in this situation becomes the environmental activist telling the vegan what they should be doing, with no intention of doing it themselves. It is all designed to silence the vegan. They will suggest more extreme measures than the vegan was advocating. If they are actually following their own advice then they should be able to advocate for it and provide practical advice in avoiding whatever problems or issues they are highlighting. After all, this is what vegans do, they highlight a problem but also provide a reasonable and practical solution and are very willing to help and offer advice if asked.

It can be useful to try and take a step back from these discussions too if they are becoming too personal. Are the things they are suggesting you should be doing things they are advocating everybody should be doing? If not, why are they targeting vegans who are already doing something? If the intention is to shame into silence then it is not so puzzling. If they are advocating it generally then how are they different from vegan activists advocating for veganism in that they are advocating for individual and population change also, just in a different area?

Of course it's not really about what everybody should be doing at all if they are opposed to advocating for change. The result they really want is the same as the ones who are 'merchants of doubt' – that is for you or onlookers to despair and think you can't possible meet such high demands for consistency and give up. What they would actually be happy with is silencing vegans, stopping the advocacy and being left in peace. If vegans can't live up to their demands, then why should they be expected to do anything? We are all hypocrites so why bother?' is how the reasoning goes. If they offer advice we can ask whether it is what they do themselves and whether they expect others to be able to do it also. Why is it acceptable for them to advocate for something, but not vegans?

When it is vegans that are using the hypocrisy arguments in the tu-quoque sense I find it useful to ask them what their case for being vegan is and if they advocate it to others and want other people to be vegan. It often reveals answers that are little to do with animal rights, animal interests, or the moral status of animals. It may also revealed that they aren't interested in advocating for others to be vegan, they are more in line with the 'personal choice' attitude that says 'each to their own'. If we are making a case for veganism then the arguments for that case have to come from the nature and sentience of animals, the ways in which they are exploited and animal rights theory. A recent unfortunate trend is to conflate veganism with a diet. If vegans are arguing with you that veganism is nothing new and has existed in cultures for thousands of years we have to ask if they are talking about plant-based diets or animal rights and veganism. Which arguments are they using from the existence of heavily plant-based cultures in favour of veganism in our current world? Certainly arguments for land management, environmentalism and use of a wide variety of plant species can be marshalled. These represent practical outcomes rather than first principles however. The arguments for a case for veganism have to be as objective and universal as possible. If they are based on specific reasons from religions or cultures are they universally applicable? Can we build a case for veganism from the reasons certain cultures were predominately plant-based? It depends on why they were plant-based. If the reasons are applicable to the current exploitation of animals and a movement to end their use then those same arguments can be used even now in a different time and place. If not, they don't get us as far as a case for veganism. Once again, the question to ask troublesome vegans is why they are vegan and see what arguments they marshal and whether they stand up to scrutiny. If they are good arguments for being vegan then at least it highlights where the disagreements may actually lie.

A tip I saw on Vegan Sidekick was to ask people who criticise an advocacy method what you should be saying and then they can repeat that back to themselves and convince themselves of the argument. If they have better arguments and advocacy methods you can learn from these and adopt what is useful.

Veganism is not enough!

Vegetarians advocate 'as far as vegetarianism' and vegans advocate as far as veganism. A vegan could only be accused of hypocrisy if they were actually vegetarian whilst advocating veganism to everyone else. So this isn't what is meant by hypocrisy at all. It's a misunderstanding of what veganism claims to address and conflating it with environmentalism. If we are using environmental arguments then we should still be clear about the claims we are making and in which areas. Beyond those areas other things have to be advocated for separately.

People already think veganism is extreme but the critics want us to believe that if vegans did put into practice their more extreme suggestions beyond the scope of veganism that these wouldn't just add further to the perception of veganism as extreme. Vegans understand that people still have lives to lead and aren't setting the bar unreasonably high. But in searching for gotchas, anti-vegans continually set the bar higher and move the goal further away. A selection of their suggestions for what vegans should be doing 'if they were serious' is not driving, using any transport, living in huts, not using the internet, not using a phone, not walking anywhere and restricting their calorie intake to the bare minimum. The reasons for these are a mixture of ideas about reducing impact on animals. Considering eliminating meat and dairy is one of the biggest steps an individual can take and one vegans have already taken shouldn't the critics have already done this? The other steps we can take for the environment are good and can be done in addition to veganism but in the area of food you should be eliminating meat and dairy and then worrying about further refining which plant foods are best if you are able. Can you imagine if vegans actually did the things they suggest we should do? We are in a no-win situation with such critics because we ware damned if we do and damned if we don't.

Anti-vegans use the sniper tactics here of demanding more consistency and then depending on how it is answered they may say it is not enough or too extreme. This is why it's a good idea to get them to state explicitly what it is they are advocating. They already know you are advocating veganism but you can't be sure what exactly they are suggesting everyone – (or is it just vegans?) – should be doing. Their advice on what vegans should be doing 'if they wanted to be more consistent' really misses the mark because vegans aren't claiming anything beyond veganism when advocating for veganism.

'Are those shoes leather?' is their call for consistency but then they get confused when it is explained that veganism is this attempt at greater consistency. It's rare that the sniper-troll has a positive position they are advocating for themselves because their position could be subject to the exact same criticisms and tactics they use.

Veganism is too much!

Critics of veganism who are not vegan often position it as extreme and too much. They distance vegans themselves and the philosophy and practice of veganism as far away from themselves as possible to exaggerate the changes that would be needed and give themselves more reassurance that it would be too difficult if the goal is too lofty or the people too ascetic.

There are vegans who do this too for their own purposes. Generally they are those who support various forms of Reducetarianism, flexetarianism, and other meat reduction strategies etc. It serves their purpose to position vegans as extremists and purists to bolster arguments about veganism being too much. Rather than work to normalise veganism in terms of attitudes and practice and normalise vegans as being regular folk they will play into negative stereotypes and reinforce false narratives about vegans and veganism.

A society thinks veganism is extreme in proportion to how normalised violence against animals has become. Reducetarians do not work to bust any myths surrounding veganism. To promote their own ideas they are willing to perpetuate harmful stereotypes and stigmas surrounding vegans rather than challenging these. Positioning vegans as terrorists and extremists puts vegan individuals who are peaceful protestors in danger. This seems to be a case of the reducetarians and 'reducetarian vegans' not having assimilated the vegan arguments fully themselves. They have given up promoting or never tried to promote veganism and make a case for veganism. In the case of non-vegan reducetarians they pay lip service to the idea of reducing to zero and 'being vegan' but have not made any serious progress along this road themselves. Perhaps for the promotion of reducetarianism they need to maintain this idea of a journey whilst never reaching the state of being vegan. They surely know all the arguments for veganism but haven't persuaded themselves to be vegan. If they are promoting reducetarianism as a gateway to veganism then they haven't followed that pathway themselves and are stuck on a plateau.

Wittgenstein's Ladder is an idea from philosopher Ludwig Wittgenstein about a ladder being useful for those that need it to climb to a certain level but then 'when he has used them (propositions)—as steps—to climb beyond them. (He must, so to speak, throw away the ladder after he has climbed up it.)

Perhaps they are maintaining the idea of the ladder or bridge to veganism which people who have actually gone vegan no longer require for themselves. However vegans already offer help, advice and guidance and offer the arguments to take people 'as far as' being vegan. Promoting the idea of a ladder maintains comfortable plateaus where there are periods of no progress and further entrenches stereotypes and myths such as animal welfare and humane slaughter. Veganism is the position that argues against these 'stages' such as reducetarianism, vegetarianism etc. A Reducetarian has no inclination to offer these arguments, particularly if they wish to maintain their 'ladder' and be in a constant state of limbo. Perhaps some are eating fully plant based in private but must maintain the reducetarian position in public as this is what they promote. Are there examples of reducetarians that have gone vegan? Certainly the leaders of the Reducetarian movement have not gone vegan even after half a decade. It's not so much about how people go vegan but about what is the correct position and principle to be advocating for as the goal.

If people believe Reducetarianism is the best way then I don't know why they call themselves vegan as they obviously do not make the case for being vegan. Why not just promote their own way and not make vegan claims? They are in the strange position of promoting reducing and saying to be vegan. How do they choose what to promote at any given time or what to promote first and to which people? If you are making a case for being vegan then a Reducetarian movement is redundant as vegans will already encourage reducing towards a definite goal and of course encourage this as soon as possible. The vegan will not accept non-vegan arguments however otherwise they would not be vegan. A Reducetarian may accept any number of anti-vegan arguments. It is also a nebulous idea with such a broad concept of 'reducing'. **Thanks For The Advice on Vegan Advocacy Person-Who-Hasn't-Even-Convinced-Themselves-To-Be-Vegan**

'Ending the battle between vegans and everyone else' clearly means vegans surrendering making a case for being vegan. (14) Brian Kateman, the founder of the Reducetarian movement, reinforces crude stereotypes and positions veganism as extreme. Vegans and those interested in minimising animal use and slaughter should be working to normalise veganism. If they don't it is because they want to distance vegans and veganism.

The author Geoff Thompson has a saying - 'no growth in comfort'. We are not seeking comfortable resting places on our 'personal journeys' where people can retreat to more thought terminating cliches, bad arguments and positions that justify the exploitation and slaughter of animals. We want to challenge these positions and make a case for veganism. Those who don't have other motives and are not making a case for being vegan. They should be honest about this and the reasons they aren't making a case for being vegan. Vegans are the ones in the unique position to make a case for being vegan.

Maybe *veganism* is a baby step!

At the other end of the spectrum there are those that think veganism is 'not enough'. This area of discussion is another one prone to Nirvana fallacies and relative privation. If the scope and focus of veganism is understood and a charitable interpretation applied then it isn't really hard to understand. (15)

This is not to say veganism is the be all and end all and solves every problem. Veganism properly understood has a definite focus – the exploitation of other animals. If you want to avoid animal exploitation and slaughter veganism is the result, whatever you wanted to call it.
Calling veganism something else doesn't make problems

with the vegan label disappear. If we still need a descriptor to describe and promote a certain philosophy it is going to come up against the same difficulties no matter what the chosen label or the areas it covers.

If there are positions that say it is too much and too little the point is not that veganism is an ideal middle ground or plateau of its own. It's that the too much and too little narratives are distortions of veganism. This is often an intentional strawman argument in order to argue against it more effectively. Veganism is either reduced too far to a consumer activity to argue that it doesn't go far enough. Or it is expanded to areas it never claimed to solve and blamed for not solving all issues of animal suffering in the world. Rather than a charitable interpretation of the definition it is distorted. No definition is going to be perfect. No definition of human rights can survive the assault of extreme pedantry and bad faith interpretations. The same is true for veganism. Pretending you don't know that the focus is animal use by humans and reasonably interpreting this as the understanding of veganism is disingenuous.

No labels.

If people don't want to be labelled or defined at all we face the problem of having to describe your position in detail each time.

Critics that say veganism is not enough tend to identify as a sort of 'meta-vegan' that has moved beyond the bounds of veganism.

Things to ask them include 'which forms of animal use and slaughter do you support and why? If you don't why not?' This should establish their position. Then if they are advocating for greater personal change than being vegan that is up to them to advocate for. If they are arguing against areas of veganism for animal use or consumption these are usually loophole areas and don't convey a strong anti-speciesist message. What are the practical solutions? Calling yourself an 'anti-speciesist' doesn't make problems in other areas that veganism is criticised for disappear. Should an 'anti-speciesist' drive or use electricity? These other areas of harm to animals are still there no matter if veganism is avoided by calling yourself something else or not being vegan. Activists that see anti-speciesism as the most important thing to promote and see veganism as an obstacle tend to commit this fallacy. They try to 'miss out' the practice of veganism or advocating that to promote activism itself instead. This skips the part where you actually address animal exploitation and slaughter and avoid it. Of course if they are vegan activists advocating for these other areas too then that is better and has the force of modelling the world of no animal exploitation. Veganism may be a baby step itself into a wider range of issues, but it's still a necessary step. 'Total Liberation' includes other animals, it does not dismiss them or place them in a hierarchy where their issues are never addressed.

Troublesome vegans may argue for reduction of meat and dairy rather than make a case for veganism and further mischaracterise the argument as **'not being all or nothing'**. This is supposed to mean it is better to do something than nothing at all. I think most vegans would agree it is better to do something rather than nothing at all. Indeed, that idea forms the basis of replies to the Nirvana fallacies we have discussed. It is usually the anti-vegan position to say perfection or 'all' in this case, can't be reached and so it is not worthwhile. The only people I have seen using all or nothing arguments are reducetarian vegans and anti-vegans arguing for positions other than veganism. Apologist vegans often end up using the same arguments as anti-vegans and seem to think any vegan advocacy is 'forcing ideas' and that everyone is on a 'journey' and it is all a matter of 'personal choice'. It's hard to see how they can make a case for veganism with such warped views of it. Characterising veganism as 'all' they are the ones saying they or others will therefore do nothing. Of course any steps towards veganism should be encouraged but a clear goal has to be set and it should be clear which positions are actually arguing for some form or another of animal use and slaughter still. Similarly, there is often an argument used saying that '**the perfect is the enemy of the good**' and this is meant to argue for positions that are 'less than' veganism. Veganism is positioned as 'perfect' and the 'good' is doing something. Making an effort or avoiding one area of animal use – essentially any of the many Reducetarian positions. The simple answer to this point is 'okay, I won't let the perfect be the enemy of the good!' But more seriously the problem is equally if the 'good' is allowed to become the enemy of the better – or any progress. It's another attempt to prevent vegan advocacy. Any advocacy for a position beyond the already 'good' could be seen as letting perfectionism be an 'enemy'. But no vegans are saying they are 'perfect' or that veganism itself is 'perfect' or 'purist', 'dogmatic' or any of those descriptors. These are mischaracterisations of a position that is practically achievable and more in line with the Nirvana fallacies presented by anti-vegans. 'Don't let the 'good' be the enemy of the 'better'! If troublesome vegans are characterising veganism as a perfect state that can be reached then they are wrong.

Without analysing the perfect/good argument it merely becomes another thought terminating cliché.

Perfection myths also lead into areas of arguments like 'Nobody Is Vegan'. The best article I have come across on this is on **Towards Freedom**. (16)

'If we liken veganism to light and non-veganism to dark, we can see that while there is no absolute light or dark, there is a very apparent and obvious difference between light and dark, which we can easily identify. There are also degrees of light and degrees of dark. Let those degrees, in the analogy, equal the degrees of practice of veganism or non-veganism. Then we see the uselessness in saying that because absolute light does not exist, noon-day light is no different or brighter than dawn light.'

There's no ethical consumption under capitalism' actually just means there is no *absolute* ethical consumption under capitalism.

Ignoring *relative* differences in degree is to commit a 'fallacy of the gray'. This fallacy arises from the often correct observation that 'things are not black and white' but replacing a two colour view of the world with a one colour view. Saying there is *no* spectrum of choices from awful to least bad is to say all choices are grey and admit no gradation of grey from almost black to almost white with infinite degrees of shading in between.

Basically by any criterion you care to mention, oat milk is more ethical than cow's or goat's milk. Products not tested on animals are more ethical than products tested on animals (all other variables being equal). It's also a Nirvana fallacy to dismiss a realistic and practical option (Veganism) because it doesn't meet the standards of a theoretical perfect solution.

We see how the ideas of absolute and relative manifestations of an idea link Nirvana fallacies, relative privation, criticisms of veganism being 'too much' or 'too little', ideas of the 'perfect' and the 'good' and 'where to draw the line'. Line drawing comes up in terms of veganism being too much/too little because the demarcation area of veganism represents too much or too little depending on the position of the person making the criticism.

A proper understanding of what veganism is and the areas it covers can clear up a lot of the misconceptions and clarify such line drawing criticisms. From the perspective of 'too little' it is a criticism of not eliminating all causes of suffering to animals in the world. Such critics point to how energy production, transport, plant agriculture, housing developments, and wild animal suffering (WAS) are still causes of death and suffering to animals. On this understanding 'veganism' represents a Utilitarian attempt to eliminate or minimise suffering. However if we understand the aim of veganism as clearly defined and the focus being on human exploitation of other animals then the criticism is unfair. When the area veganism covers is understood such criticisms are merely saying 'veganism does not address or cover the areas it doesn't cover'. There are indeed numerous causes of animal suffering outside of the focus of veganism. But it's an uncharitable view to say veganism is not worthwhile because it doesn't address these areas. There aren't areas of animal exploitation that veganism claims to cover but does not. Of course the argument can and should be made to address these other areas. It is when they are used to dismiss veganism that it is an issue. Plastic use, transport and energy use and all the questions that impact animals are questions for everyone, not just vegans. If the problem is being pointed out then we should expect a practical solution to be offered also. Veganism identifies a problem and also gives practical advice and guidance on avoiding it and using alternatives. Vegans also practice what they preach. It is to be hoped those advocating for other areas do the same.

Sometimes these criticisms are a conflation of veganism with environmentalism. There is an environmental aspect to veganism but it is still those areas that are to do with current animal use and the alternatives to animal use and their environmental impact. The fact that humans can't have zero impact on the total environment isn't an argument against veganism. Food production is an obvious area of environmental impact that is relevant to veganism.

Other areas such as plastic use are relevant but require improving on their own terms. As a variable it does not help to consume plastic wrapped animal products or remove plastic use but still consume animal products that are much worse for the environment. Alongside veganism we can work on these other areas. Once again, there is no false dilemma, no fallacy of relative privation. Many vegan companies are more conscious of the need to reduce and eliminate environmentally harmful practices.

Animals First. Animals Last.

With the fallacy of relative privation we saw how invoking bigger problems doesn't negate the validity of 'smaller' problems. As vegans we are used to answering criticisms such as 'why don't you care about human rights issues?' or about prioritising other problems in the world. We usually answer that we don't have to set up a hierarchy because we can care about more than one issue simultaneously. We can be vegan and care about human rights. Indeed, many of us were fighting for disability rights and other issues before we became vegan and so continue to advocate for those having added other animals covered by veganism to our areas of concern. What we want is for people who are fighting for whatever issues to also add in veganism and vice versa.
Unfortunately there are some vegans who could be termed 'animals first' who have said things like 'I don't care about your rights if you don't care about animal rights'. This is in effect an inverse of the fallacious position of the anti-vegan who says 'I don't care about animal rights if you don't care about the issue I'm advocating for'. Rather than recognising how we normally answer criticism by saying we can are about more than one issue at a time they are promoting the idea that they actually do only care about one issue.

This is not to say it doesn't swing too far the other way either with an 'animals last' approach where any discussion of animal rights will always be derailed or where granting moral consideration to animals is deferred until all human problems are solved i.e. never. Thinking about the 'focus and scope' of veganism to borrow a phrase from Roger Yates can help us here. Animals and how they are exploited is and should be the focus of veganism but the scope of veganism expands to cover so many other areas, as we have seen with discussions on environmental racism, slaughterhouse workers. Plus, it remains a fact that it is humans doing the animal exploitation and it is humans we are advocating too. So any issues around accessibility and putting veganism into practice need to be addressed and solved as it is human attitudes and behaviour towards other animals that needs to change.

''We can't change the world for animals without changing our ideas about animals. We have to move from the idea that animals are things, tools, machines, commodities, resources here for our use..to the idea that as sentient beings they have their own inherent value and dignity.'' - Andrew Linzey via Evolve! Campaigns

There are risks with every type of advocacy. I don't think the hardest questions come from outside criticisms of veganism but from 'within' veganism. How best to advocate and how best to shift society to veganism in practical terms for example.

Summary

I believe this guide offers the general outline of a framework that most arguments raised when veganism is the topic can fit into. When an argument arises you can categorise it into whether it is in the area of ethics, the environment or health. You can analyse the arguments to see if they are psychological and emotional responses or whether they attempt to use logic to prove set of premises. Further we can see what facts are available and debunk any misinformation and myths. Veganism is as easy or as hard to understand as you want to make it. If you really want to take a deep dive you will be learning about evolution, agriculture, and animal sentience, how animals are used, plant biology, philosophy, religions, ethics, nutrition, environment and climate change. I can't think of many single topics that touch on so any areas in fact, probably because people want to marshal arguments from all these areas against you! I don't think it is really a hard concept to grasp and that most of the questions aren't really genuine sources of confusion or sincerely held beliefs. When people are strongly motivated to maintain a positive view of themselves and ease any possible cognitive dissonance it can lead to adopting absurd positions to try to argue against veganism. If vegans are bad then they can maintain an idea of being good despite supporting animal slaughter and exploitation. There must be something wrong with veganism rather than the human domination and commodification of animals and slaughter on an unimaginable scale.

The guide started with thought terminating clichés, a way not to discuss the topic at all, perhaps because it is too uncomfortable but also because of misconceptions of veganism. Types of discussion followed where we can more easily analyse whether our discussion is going to be beneficial by following certain etiquette and how many types of low-grade non-arguments can simply be ignored as they are low on Graham's hierarchy. Types of evidence and argument can become more relevant and of higher quality. This is when it gets interesting and where the person arguing may not want to get into because it means adopting more premises and committing to an actual position that has to be defended. We are now in the territory of having to practice what you preach. There is always an option to go nuclear or use various escape hatches to once again get out of a serious discussion. At this stage however if arguments are being offered they can finally be analysed for truth-value. Many arguments will be logical fallacies, most often due to irrelevance. Thinking about the variables in arguments can help us greatly in identifying the most important factors that lead to sound arguments. Other arguments will be attempts to actually engage with the issues raised by veganism. These become better arguments because they are relevant ad are looking at the data we have available. They may be attempts at 'gotcha' questions for vegans and finding loopholes that circumvent the usual way of production. The irony of many of these arguments is how they backfire with greater force. By trying to use these type of arguments the premises of the arguments for veganism are accepted and trying to find where there may be 'exceptions to the rule' actually only serves to 'prove the rule'. For example, finding instances of absolute necessity for killing an animal to survive merely highlights the ways it is unnecessary in every other circumstance. In analysing these arguments we see that they can often be turned around and what seemed like a gotcha only strengthens the case for veganism. This brought us to the next category and what I call 'reflexive arguments' where the premises of veganism are accepted but a slightly different conclusion is reached. Again this can backfire because if they have miscalculated their argument they are proving the case for veganism themselves. If they are actually committed to the argument they should be following their own advice. Reflexive arguments are best thought of as following a path 99% of the way but then taking a U-Turn in the road at the end. People like to argue this 1% fork in the road without walking all the way up to 99% themselves. Most arguments against veganism backfire due to ecological efficiency. They are the equivalent of people trying to demonstrate a perpetual motion machine that contravenes the laws of thermodynamics. Scalability of attempted loopholes in the usual energy transfer between trophic levels renders them only ever applicable in very specific circumstances, exceptional cases and small percentages of how humans actually obtain animal products.

A strange thing happens as the arguments become more relevant and accept more premises if the person is still hostile to veganism and doesn't actually commit to following their own recommendations – the arguments become more disingenuous and dishonest. Whilst the taste of animal flesh isn't a great argument for inflicting massive suffering on animals, at least it is honest. Many of the 'early on' arguments are more honest and of this straightforward nature. Later on arguments become more sophisticated but less honest and people are no longer actually following the consequences and implications of their arguments. It's at this stage people are realising the traditional bad arguments haven't worked or are fallacies so they attempt to employ other talking points. There can be problems with types of vegan advocacy but there is nothing inherently 'problematic' about veganism itself. Animals are victims and should be acknowledged as having interests. This is not changed by any arguments about vegan advocacy methods.

The seven stages of grief play a part in the progression of the arguments I believe. I think there is a massive amount of grief when we confront animal exploitation and face up to its reality. The first stage is Shock and denial. This is a state of disbelief and numbed feelings. Here is where thought terminating clichés and denialism of all sorts emerge

Pain and guilt. ...

Anger and bargaining. ... anger directed at vegans,
Shooting the messenger. Bargaining is manifested as trying to maintain the idea of 'humane slaughter', animal 'welfare' within a system of exploitation and slaughter and bargaining with environmental offsets and attempts to say it is better for the environment to use animals.
Depression. ... sadness and despair, feeling hopeless
The upward turn. ...
Reconstruction and working through. ...
Acceptance and hope – doing something about it, being an example of how we can model the future we want.
Restoring a fair relationship with other animals.

The Ethical Omnivore Movement is a late stage example of this bargaining. If they were serious they would be arguing just as vigorously against those who indiscriminately consume any and all animal products as they do against vegans. They would be advocating for a minimisation of animal slaughter because they would recognise that this is required to meet their goal of minimising harm and impact. In fact they should be supporting vegans because there is no way their model can scale to population levels, it just isn't feasible whether those solutions are hunting, eating roadkill or regenerative agriculture for which there is not enough land .The rest of the population apart from those who were actually following their recommendations would have to be vegan. (17) This constitutes almost as large a shift towards more plant-based options and a shift towards plant based diets as veganism represents. It's not an argument for the status quo so why is it used that way and why are vegans targeted rather than the areas of animal use and consumption that would absolutely have to disappear if they want to approach towards that crossover area of where they think they are claiming to minimise impact and where vegans are minimising impact. I've never seen vegetarians or ethical omnivores help out vegans in arguments against all these areas that they say they want abolished too. Vegans are the ones putting forward the case for this abolition and should be supported in all those areas.

Understanding veganism.

Veganism is NOT a diet. Veganism is the principle of not exploiting and commodifying animals for human use. It follows from this principle that we do not use animals for a food source and so follow a fully plant-based diet. Our diet makes up the most significant impact on how animals are used and so most of the animal exploitation we want to avoid is diet related. Eating is the thing we do most often that is a continuous choice whereas the impact on animals from manufacturing one-off purchases is not as large. However veganism is more than just the diet as animals are used for clothing, transport, cosmetics and entertainment. Veganism is NOT environmentalism, in the same way it is not a diet. Veganism impacts the environment so environmentalism forms an important area of concern. It is however a misconception that leads discussions astray to think veganism is about 'saving the environment'. To be sure plant-based diets can have a lower environmental impact and should be a part of any environmentalists concern but veganism has animal exploitation as its focus. Veganism is a movement to end animal exploitation, end the property status of animals and recognise their moral status. It should follow from recognising animals as sentient individuals that they have moral status and should therefore be free from exploitation from humans. The burden of proof should be on those who want to confine and kill animals when there is no good justification for doing so. The extremely weak arguments against veganism do not provide a case for subjecting animals to the exploitation and slaughter that they are victims of. Veganism is hated because it brings into sharp contrast the pretence of 'respect' for animals and claims of 'welfare' with the alternative of a real paradigm shift in our relationship with animals. In challenging human supremacism it evokes strong reactions. If we think about the idea of 'welfare' with any honesty, we see that it is still within the paradigm of using animals and has only ever been the bare minimum required. (18)

My own reasons for being vegan are that it is a practice of my desire to minimise impact on other animals by not supporting their exploitation and slaughter.

One of the strongest cases I have read for veganism is Mylan Engel Jnr's 'The Immorality of Eating Meat' and I urge all readers to examine that argument. (19) I agree with Leslie Cross that we as humans greatly erred in exploiting other animals and veganism represents a step in correcting this historical wrong. (20) It is my position that animal agriculture and other forms of animal exploitation are essentially canned hunting but utilising different species. If I would object to canned hunting or dogs being slaughtered and through species overlap can't find any morally relevant differences between pigs and dogs then I can't justify exploiting and slaughtering pigs. I carry on this process for all animal species that are sentient and therefore have moral status and interests. I think animals have worth irrespective of their utility to humans. Anti-vegan arguments are not good enough to justify the exploitation and slaughter of other animals and offer no firm reason why I shouldn't be vegan and avoid the vast majority of animal exploitation and slaughter as there are alternatives available to me.

Ask yourself what are your criteria for extending moral consideration to animals. Which forms of animal use and slaughter do you already definitely oppose and why? Can this principle be extended to more areas and more species? There is no doubt that we discriminate against certain individuals purely because of their species. This is a

prejudice based of externalities and irrelevant variables and ignores the morally relevant scientific facts.
I will leave the last word to the great Al-Ma'arri (December 973 – May 1057) an Arab philosopher, poet, and writer whose voice is as relevant now as it was over a Millenium ago when he was writing. (21) Recognising the kleptoparasitism inherent in human relations with other species (stealing milk, honey and food) and the unjust nature of human exploitation of other animals he states how he wish he had reformed his relationship with other animals before he had grown old, a refrain echoed by millions of vegans as their only regret ever since –

'I wish I had gone vegan sooner!'

I no longer steal from Nature

You are diseased in understanding and religion.
Come to me, that you may hear something of sound truth.
Do not unjustly eat fish the water has given up,
And do not desire as food the flesh of slaughtered animals,
Or the white milk of mothers who intended its pure draught for their young, not noble ladies.
And do not grieve the unsuspecting birds by taking eggs;
for injustice is the worst of crimes.
And spare the honey which the bees get industriously from the flowers of fragrant plants;
For they did not store it that it might belong to others,
Nor did they gather it for bounty and gifts.
I washed my hands of all this; and wish that I
Perceived my way before my hair went gray!

Al-Ma'arri

Notes to Chapter Seven

(1). https://www.livescience.com/39481-time-to-declare-animal-sentience.html
(2) https://www.smithsonianmag.com/science-nature/fish-feel-pain-180967764/#:~:text=Moreover%2C%20the%20notion%20that%20fish,subjective%20experience%20of%20the%20world
(3) https://fcmconference.org/img/CambridgeDeclarationOnConsciousness.pdf
(4) https://www.unenvironment.org/resources/report/preventing-future-zoonotic-disease-outbreaks-protecting-environment-animals-and
(5) https://www.truthordrought.com/infectious-diseases
(6) https://plantbaseddata.medium.com/preventing-the-next-pandemic-the-role-of-animal-agriculture-and-destruction-of-nature-1bb297aa3941
(7) https://www.who.int/foodsafety/areas_work/antimicrobial-resistance/amrfoodchain/en/#:~:text=The%20high%20volume%20of%20antibiotics,the%20amount%20used%20in%20humans.
(8) https://pubmed.ncbi.nlm.nih.gov/27886704/
List of statements on vegan diets.
https://theresanelephantintheroomblog.wordpress.com/2016/11/10/in-a-nutshell-a-plant-based-diet-and-health/
(9) http://advances.nutrition.org/content/7/6/1005.abstract
Public Library of Science -
http://journals.plos.org/plosone/article?id=10.1371%2Fjournal.pone.0165797
(10) Phosphorus use / Fertilisers
- https://phys.org/news/2017-03-phosphorus-vital-life-earth-runninglow.html
(11) https://www.sbs.com.au/topics/science/earth/article/2016/02/19/how-great-phosphorus-shortage-could-leave-us-all-hungry
(12) https://www.nature.com/articles/ncomms10696
Further reading -
https://www.jstor.org/stable/26427710?seq=1#metadata_info_tab_contents
https://www.ncbi.nlm.nih.gov/pmc/articles/PMC5001165/
https://www.npr.org/sections/thesalt/2013/02/14/172009950/should-you-be-worried-about-your-meats-phosphorus-footprint?t=1599167727738

https://phys.org/news/2016-02-great-phosphorus-shortage-short-food.html#jCp

(13) Shelley - http://www.animal-rights-library.com/texts-c/shelley01.htm

(14) https://www.youtube.com/watch?v=yJJtRWFL_gw

(15) https://onhumanrelationswithothersentientbeings.weebly.com/the-blog/veganisms-defining-issues-focus-scope

(16) http://www.towardsfreedom.com/292.html

(17) https://www.bloomberg.com/news/features/2020-12-17/saving-the-amazon-starts-with-cleaning-up-the-beef-industry?fbclid=IwAR1VguHcPqGnrpsnZ1648u7mtcKMsCMG0TAgsmdKIpitxw4ELRQFvTrYUdQ

(18) https://edenfarmedanimalsanctuary.com/veganism/

(19) https://philpapers.org/archive/ENGTIO-16.pdf

(20) http://www.candidhominid.com/p/vegan-story.html

(21) Adapted from "Studies in Islamic Poetry" by Reynold A. Nicholson, Cambridge University Press, 1921 via Vegan Good Life

Further Reading

There are many more resources and scientific papers available at the Plant Based Data, a website compiled and managed by Dr. Tushar Mehta, M.D., Nicholas Carter, M.A. and Nital Jethalal, MSc
https://www.plantbaseddata.org/

EAT Lancet report - https://eatforum.org/eat-lancet-commission/

IPCC REPORT -
https://www.ipcc.ch/site/assets/uploads/2019/08/2f.-Chapter-5_FINAL.pdf

Food and Climate Research Network -
https://www.futureoffood.ox.ac.uk/article/food-climate-research-network
Chatham House
https://www.chathamhouse.org/topics/agriculture-and-food
Our World in Data
https://ourworldindata.org/environmental-impacts-of-food
Truth or Drought
https://www.truthordrought.com/myths-overview
Food Empowerment Project - https://foodispower.org

Select Bibliography

On Their Own Terms by Lee Hall

Eating Earth by Lisa Kemmerer

Meat Logic by Charles Horn

Mind If I Order The Cheeseburger?: And Other Questions People Ask Vegans by Sherry F. Colb

Farm to Fable: The Fictions of our Animal-Consuming Culture by Robert Grillo

Five Essays for Freedom: A political primer for animal advocates by Kristy Alger

Printed in Great Britain
by Amazon